RESTORING
PRAISE
& WORSHIP
TO THE ✝ CHURCH

An Anthology of Articles on

RESTORING
PRAISE
& WORSHIP
TO THE ✝ CHURCH

Editors:
David Blomgren
Dean Smith
Douglas Christoffel

All Scripture references are from the King James Version, unless otherwise indicated. AMP = Amplified Bible (New Testament c. The Lockman Foundation 1954, 1958; Old Testament c. Zondervan Publishing House 1962, 1964); NASB = New American Standard Bible (c. The Lockman Foundation 1960, 1962, 1963, 1968, 1971, 1972, 1973, 1975, 1977); NIV = New International Version (c. New York International Bible Society 1970, 1973, 1975, 1976, 1977, 1978); NKJV = New King James Version (c. Thomas Nelson Inc., Publishers 1979, 1980, 1982).

"Restoring Praise & Worship"
Editors: David K. Blomgren
Dean Smith
& Doug Christoffel

Published and printed by:

Revival Press

Worship and Praise Division
of
Destiny Image Publishers
P.O. Box 351
Shippensburg, PA 17257

ISBN 0-938612-40-9

For Worldwide Distribution
Printed in the U.S.A.

TABLE
OF CONTENTS

Chpt.	Title	Page

CONTRIBUTING
AUTHORS

DR. DAVID K. BLOMGREN pastors Tampa Bay Christian Center in Brandon, Florida. He is the editor of "Restoration Today Magazine." He holds a B.A. degree from Tennessee Temple University, a M.A. degree from the University of Portland, the M.Div., Th.M. and D.Min. degrees from Western Conservative Baptist Seminary and a Th.D. degree from Logos Graduate School. As a conference and seminar speaker, Dr. Blomgren has ministered throughout North America and in many foreign countries. He has authored numerous books, including *The Song of the Lord, Prophetic Gatherings,* and the best-seller, *Restoring God's Glory.*

LARRY DEMPSEY is an Executive Director of the International Worship Symposium, prolific teacher and writer, musical composer and unity advocate. He and his wife Joan travel in full-time teaching ministry. He is the founder of Royal Priesthood Ministries in Santa Ana, California, U.S.A.

CLEMENT J. FERRIS is well known as a Bible teacher and has a prophetic ministry. He is on staff and serves as a worship leader at Tampa Bay Christian Center in Brandon, Florida. He has taught worship seminars throughout the United States and in several foreign countries.

DR. DAVID E. FISCHER is Associate Pastor of Living Waters Temple in Pasadena, California, U.S.A. He is director of Living Word Institute of Worship and is on the Board of Directors of the International Worship Symposium. As well as being an accomplished trumpet player and worship leader, Dr. Fischer has an international ministry as a worship and praise conference speaker.

ARLENE FRIESEN has been a music instructor at Christ For the Nations Institute in Dallas, Texas for 12 years and is currently serving as Interim Chairman of the Music Department. For several years she also served as Music Director at a Bible school in Germany and has travelled throughout northern Europe and in other nations in music ministry. In recent years her concern for children has led her to become actively involved in, and to speak in behalf of, music ministry to children.

REV. ERNEST GENTILE has been active in pastoral, teaching and prophetic ministry for the past forty years. He speaks frequently at ministers' seminars, camp meetings and churches in the U.S. As well, he has ministered in nine foreign countries. He founded Christian Community Church in San Jose, California, U.S.A., twenty-eight years ago. This church sponsors both an academy (K-12) and a Bible college.

REV. DWIGHT GREINER is senior pastor of Meadow Lake Christian Centre in Meadow Lake, Sask., Canada. He was sent out from Maranatha Christian Centre (Regina, Sask.) in 1985 where he had been on pastoral and Bible school staff for six years. He writes regularly for *Restoration Magazine* through a column on Supportive Ministry. He and his wife, Roberta, have 4 children.

BARRY GRIFFING is Minister of Worship at Tabernacle Church in Melbourne, Florida, U.S.A. He is currently directing the establishment of a worship training center in his home church and is also a director for the International Worship Symposium. He is the founder of Zion Song Ministries and is a renowned musician and seminarian in the area of praise and worship.

STEVE GRIFFING is Director of Music at Fountain Gate Ministries in Plano, Texas, U.S.A., where he has founded a School of Music to train anointed worship leaders and music directors. He is also Dean of the International Worship Symposium. As a violinist, conductor, music teacher and Bible expositor he has inspired Christians and congregations across the U.S. to worship the Lord with excellence.

MIKE HERRON is pastor of Wilamette Valley Christian Fellowship in Salem, Oregon. He was formerly an elder at Bible Temple, taught at their Bible College and was Chief Musician there for nine years. Pastor Herron has taught music seminars in South America, Europe and New Zealand, as well as in the U.S.A. and Canada.

MARK MELBY is the senior worship leader of Maranatha Christian Centre in Regina, Sask., Canada. As well as his music involvements, Bro. Mark teaches at Maranatha Training Institute and serves as the business administrator for the Centre. He has conducted a number of seminars in the area of worship and supportive ministry in churches in western Canada and as well in the U.S.

REV. ANDREW PICKLYK is senior pastor of Bible Truth Church in Kamloops, British Columbia, Canada. He has travelled as an evangelist and more recently, as a speaker at a number of church camps and leadership conferences. His church is involved in a number of ministries including a Christian academy. Bro. Picklyk and his wife, Evelyn, have 2 children.

HOWARD RACHINSKI is music minister at Bible Temple in Portland, Oregon, U.S.A. where he leads worship and directs an 80 voice choir and 30 piece orchestra. He is Director of Starpraise Ministries, a ministry developed to permit legal usage of overhead transparencies for worship songs. He is also chairman of the annual Northwest Music Ministers Conference.

BOB SORGE pastors Zion Fellowship in Canandaigua, New York, U.S.A. Previously he was Assistant to Pastors Graham and Pamela Truscott at Restoration Temple in San Diego, California, and was also formerly the Director of Music at Elim Bible Institute in Lima, New York, for three years. Pastor Sorge has hosted and taught at several worship seminars and has travelled extensively to teach and lead in worship.

DR. GRAHAM TRUSCOTT and his wife Pamela are the founders and pastors of Restoration Temple in San Diego, California, U.S.A. They spent eighteen years as missionaries in India. He is a popular speaker and his travels have taken him through forty countries. Dr. Truscott is the author of several well-known books including *The Power of His Presence*.

J. MARK WITT ministers primarily in the establishment of local churches in the country of Mexico. He also ministers in music training and conferences throughout Mexico and in the U.S.A. He and his wife, Miriam, live in Durango, Mexico, where he oversees "Project Youth," a very fruitful and active outreach ministry of his home church. A very gifted musician, Mark recently completed his first record album, which is in Spanish.

PART I

GOD'S PLAN
FOR PRAISE & WORSHIP

WORSHIP IN
THEOLOGICAL BALANCE
by Dr. David K. Blomgren

T he church universal has been experiencing great pressures for the last several years. Many churches have faced severe financial pressures, relational pressures, civil pressure against expansion, community opposition, moral problems and strong Satanic opposition. No Bible-believing, Spirit-filled church has escaped this pressure. We must ask ourselves the question, "What is God saying to the church through all of these pressures?"

One of the purposes of God through this pressure is to bring the Spirit-filled church today back into theological balance in its worship. God hates imbalance and it is an abomination to Him (Proverbs 11:1). It is God who weighs churches and individuals in the balance (Daniel 5:27; Psalm 62:9). God is weighing His church today to measure any imbalance.

How does God weigh His church in the balance? Proverbs 16:11 says, "A just weight and balance are the Lord's; all the weights of the bag are his work." This verse states that a proper balance is the work of the Lord. The word "weights" is literally "stones" in the Hebrew language (*'eben*). An imbalance was rectified in Scriptural times by putting more stones in the scale. These stones put pressure on the scale and brought it down until it was in balance with the other scale. God says that which brings the pressure is His work to bring us into balance.

What are some theological imbalances in our worship that God desires to adjust today? What imbalances in our Spirit-filled churches are there in worship which are withholding the dynamic of His power released in a greater dimension and the manifestation of His presence in a greater revelation of His glory?

Imbalance #1: An overemphasis on the *relational* at the expense of the *reverencial* in our approach to God.

This imbalance has occurred as a result of our reaction against the ritualism of high church formal worship. Our Spirit-filled churches have reacted to a dead religion that misplaced reverence by taking it out of life and putting it into liturgy, by taking it out of our spirit and putting it into sacrament, by taking it out of praise and putting it into procession. It took the focus of worship off of God Himself, who is invisible and made reverence to be seen in visible form and ceremony. It made reverence to be expressed in stained glass windows and empty symbolism.

Our reaction to dead ritual has been proper and warranted. The result has been a worship which is distinctively informal and basically unstructured. Our reaction purposed to bring worship from ritual back to the real, from liturgy to love, from litany to liberation and from ceremony to celebration. There-fore, the distinct characteristics of Spirit-filled worship have been freedom, laxness, casualness and informality. The important issue has been a relationship with God and worship as a dynamic of that relationship.

Although this is absolutely correct, the imbalance has been that much of our worship has allowed the pendulum to swing too far in the opposite direction. In much of our worship we have lost a sense of the reverence of God. True reverence is a vital ingredient in dynamic worship. Psalm 89:7 says, "God is greatly to be feared in the assembly of the saints and to be had in reverence of all them that are about Him." Reverence is a profound respect, mingled with awe and veneration. It is an homage, a recognition of honor due and an obeisance. Reverence acknowledges in Godly fear and lowly humility the high exaltation of a sovereign and holy God.

There must be a sensitive balance between reverence and comradery. Comradery is the relational aspect which approaches God as a comrade, an intimate, a friend. Certainly God is all these things to the believer, but if this relational aspect is overemphasized, all sense of reverence is lost. There are three enemies of reverence in worship which are characteristic of a relational imbalance. They are the following:

a. Familiarity. The danger in overemphasizing the perspective of God as a "comrade" is to become too familiar with God. God is simply "the Man upstairs." Our buildings are often common and our attitude towards God becomes common. We begin to view the prophetic word with a yawn or a prophetic song with a demeanor being mildly bored. There will then be no Godly fear, no sense of awe. Our concentration is on how we feel at the moment.

b. Fraternity. The danger is to fraternize rather than to fear God. God is perceived as a "Good Buddy," the Great Sidekick in the sky, a Trusty Chum, or a Pious Pal. He would be seen as there to help in time of trouble as a friend should, to be a companion, but not so much as an object of worship.

c. Flippancy. God can be so common to us that our approach is casual and even careless. A familiar children's song describes prayer as calling, "Operator, give me Heaven," on Heaven's royal telephone. The joy of the Lord is described as going down to St. Peter's bar to get "drunk as a skunk" on the Holy Ghost wine. Heaven is the great playground in the sky, the beach at the other side of Jordan where we party forever more.

We need a greater reverence for God than these attitudes reveal or we are not serving Him acceptably, "...we may serve God acceptably with reverence and godly fear. For our God is a consuming fire" (Hebrews 12:28b-29). Reverence in our worship cannot come out of emotions or hype, it can only come out of a greater understanding of God.

Imbalance #2: An overemphasis on the Immanence of God at the expense of the Transcendence of God in our worship.

These two theological truths, immanence and transcendence, must be kept in delicate balance. Transcendence teaches that God is far above man. He is "high and lifted up" (Isaiah 6:1). He is so far above man that man in his natural state could not stand in God's unveiled presence without being consumed. He is enthroned in regal splendor as sovereign Lord and man is far below Him.

Immanence teaches that God is very much involved in the affairs of man. He is a down-to-earth God. He takes care of His own and is involved in man's needs and circumstances. He comes down to us and meets us at the point of our need.

How do we understand these two concepts of God? God is transcendent as to His nature and He is immanent as to His deeds. When we overemphasize transcendence, we have a God who is disinterested, cold and impersonal. When we overemphasize immanence, we have a warm, loving God who is little more than a Divine errand boy — a God who is primarily there to serve man rather than to be served — a God who is expected to perform if He expects to receive our worship.

An imbalance in our Spirit-filled churches has caused us to have too great an appreciation for the immanence of God and far too little for His transcendence. Therefore, God is seen as too low, too mundane, a God to use instead of a God who is primarily to be exalted. Although many songs contain words about exalting God, they have often been more vernacular than veracity in our approach to worship. Some of the approach of faith formulas have become unbalanced immanence. We believe we have God in a box. He is at our service, to be used for His deeds instead of worshipped for His nature.

An evidence of this imbalance is that often our evaluation of God is based more upon His actions than upon His attributes. We value most what He does for us. We don't really revere Him for who He is as we should.

Imbalance #3: An overemphasis on the anthropocentric, or man-centered aspect at the expense of the theocentric, or God-centered aspect.

Worship must be God-centered. Worship is man's response to God's revelation of Himself. Worship begins with God and ends with Him. He owns the right to man's worship. Therefore, the focus must be away from man and directly on God. Worship is not for our benefit but for God's honor and exaltation.

The manifestation of this imbalance may be both corporate and individual. Corporately, Spirit-filled churches will sometimes try to hype a worship service, as though the whole thrust was to make us feel better. Many songs and even sermons concentrate on man and his plight without emphasizing God and His Person. The thought and intense desire of the worshipper must be fixed upon God and not upon self or the concerns of self. Therefore, true worship in balance is determined by a revelation of God.

Imbalance #4: An overemphasis on love at the expense of holiness in our approach to God.

In Spirit-filled circles there has been a preoccupation with Divine love that has caused a dangerous imbalance. This imbalance has left many with the idea that since God is a God of love, He wants His people to be blessed and prosperous at any cost.

This overemphasis and distortion of the love of God has obscured God's holiness. Some would consider God as wanting to give unlimited blessings to His creation regardless of holiness. You are unloving to say that God would judge someone for continuous sin. Church leadership is seen as unloving to exercise church discipline on an unrepentant, sinning brother. Church leaders who fall morally believe that they should take a two week vacation and continue on with their pastoral duties as before. Thus sin is reduced to a misdemeanor, iniquity to a mistake and unrighteousness to a misadventure. While an overemphasis on Divine love can move us towards license and antinomianism, an overemphasis on holiness moves us towards legalism. They must be kept in balance.

In our worship, holiness qualifies us to stand in God's presence (Psalm 24:3-4). We are called to be a "holy priesthood" (I Peter 2:5). Without a balance of Divine love and holiness, worship degenerates into our setting the standards for God instead of our submission to His standards.

Imbalance #5: An overemphasis on edification at the expense of exaltation.

Edification is an integral part of our worship services. I Corinthians 14:26b, "Let all things be done unto edifying." However, an overemphasis on the side of, "How am I doing now," or, "How do you feel now," will present a dangerous imbalance. This overemphasis on edification will cause the worshipper to wait until He feels better to worship God. Worship does not depend on how I feel now, but on the fact that God is worthy of worship no matter how I feel (Revelation 5:9). Our worship must not be based on the feelings of human nature but on the fact of His Divine nature. It must not be based on my emotions but on His essence. The attitude of the worshipper must be that worship is not for my benefit, but it is rather for Him.

This imbalance of an exaggerated concentration on edification will make a church introverted. Edification is not an end in itself, it is a means to an end. An overemphasis on edification will destroy evangelism and outreach. The danger is to concentrate so much on ourselves that we have no burden for the lost. We can become more concerned with "feeling good" than with weeping for lost souls. On the other hand, an overemphasis on evangelism at the expense of edification will sacrifice standards for statistics, quality for quantity. There must be a balance!

Exaltation must also be an integral part of our worship services. Exaltation is a Divine command, "Exalt ye the Lord our God and worship at His footstool; for He is holy" (Psalm 99:5). How can we exalt the Lord, if He is already exalted in His transcendence? There are two aspects to God's exaltation.

1. God's Intrinsic Exaltation.

This is the exaltation that He has in Himself. Psalm 97:9, "For thou, Lord, art high above all the earth: thou art exalted far above all gods." Exaltation is intrinsic in His nature. The greatness and majesty of God is not dependent on us. We don't give this exaltation to Him; it's His by virtue of who He is as God. If no one ever worshipped God, He would still be exalted.

a. The Potency of His Exaltation. His exaltation is seen in His great superiority of power. Psalm 118:16, "The right hand of the Lord is exalted..." He is far above all other powers and authorities in His potent power.

b. The Position of His Exaltation. In His stately, regal Lordship God is exalted on His throne above all others. Psalm 47:8-9, "God reigneth over the heathen: God sitteth upon the throne of his holiness...He is greatly exalted."

2. God's Extrinsic Exaltation.

This is the exaltation which is given to Him by His chosen

people. It refers to His recognized exaltation. Our praise and worship exalts Him before the world. The Psalmist said, "Thou art my God and I will praise thee: thou art my God, I will exalt thee" (Psalm 118:28). We cannot add to His nature, but we can enhance His exaltation in the eyes of the world.

a. The Revelation of His exaltation. We exalt God by lifting Him up before the unbeliever as a declaration that He is truly God and that He is all that He said He was. Extrinsic exaltation is a testimonial as His believers reveal who He is to the world. Psalm 46:10, "...I will be exalted among the heathen, I will be exalted in the earth."

b. The Recognition of His Exaltation. It is also a recognition, an acknowledgment that He is truly everything to His people that He has spoken in His Word. In our worship we confess that He is indeed exalted, Psalm 107:32, "Let them exalt Him also in the congregation of the people . . ."

The key to a healthy, dynamic, worshipping church is balance. We have seen that the catalyst of imbalance is a preoccupation with self. God is putting pressure upon the church so that these imbalances will be adjusted.

God is bringing the needed adjustments to ready us for the next mighty visitation of God. The power of that mighty outpouring will be released in dynamic worship in which His glory is manifested even greater than ever before.

2

KING DAVID'S "NEW TESTAMENT" WORSHIP
by Dr. David E. Fischer

A restoration of Biblical worship is taking place in the church of Jesus Christ in this generation as the worship expressions of the Psalms are coming alive in the twentieth century! Especially in Pentecostal and charismatic circles and also in Bible-believing churches on a wide denominational spectrum, Christians are beginning to worship the Lord with a fresh liberty and excitement. Everywhere they are testifying to a greater experience of God's presence as they praise the Lord with the lifting of hands, with clapping and rejoicing, with singing and shouting, with worship forms of the dance found in the Old Testament, with instruments and with joyful processions of praise as in Psalm 68:25!

In other words, there is a present day restoration of "Davidic worship" occurring in the church. This is the kind of worship and praise which was ordained by King David and is described

9

and commanded in the book of Psalms. Many church leaders today have received this Biblical restoration with enthusiasm, while others have wondered how a return to "Old Testament" worship forms could bring true revival to a "New Testament" church.

My purpose in this article is to set forth a New Testament basis for Davidic worship, so that churches everywhere can be encouraged to accept this area of truth. I believe we ought to throw open our windows with joy to the breath of God that is blowing on the church today as it did in the days of the Psalms. This move is bringing forth the same prophetic liberty as it did in "the days of old" (see Amos 9:11).

1. DAVID BUILT A NEW TABERNACLE ON MT. ZION, DIFFERENT FROM THE TABERNACLE OF MOSES.

Many Christians are ignorant of the fact that David even had a tabernacle! The truth is that after the Ark of the Covenant was captured by the Philistines in the days of Eli and was later returned to Israel, it was *not* replaced in the Holy of Holies in the Tabernacle of Moses! When King David recovered the ark, he put it in a new tabernacle in the city of David, which was "Zion" (see I Chronicles 15:1; 16:1; II Chronicles 5:2).

2. DAVID ORDAINED A NEW ORDER OF PRIESTHOOD FOR HIS TABERNACLE IN ZION TO PRAISE THE LORD "CONTINUALLY BEFORE THE ARK" WITH INSTRUMENTS AND SINGING.

What a revolutionary act! Under the Mosaic covenant no one was even allowed to approach the ark except the high priest, once a year. Now David ordained hundreds of singers and musicians in twenty-four rotating shifts or "courses," to praise and worship the Lord "continually before the ark" (see I Chronicles 16:4; 25:1-31). Something very significant had happened! By allowing singers and musicians to worship "before the ark," God was showing us how we could approach the glory of His presence. He showed that it need not be by the symbolic and ritualistic acts of the Tabernacle of Moses (such as the lighting of candles, the burning of incense, or the slaughter of animals), but by the simple act of praise and worship! A revolutionary new truth was revealed in the Tabernacle of David: We can "come before His presence with *singing*;" we can "enter into His gates with *thanksgiving*" and we can enter "into His courts with *praise*" (see Psalm 100).

3. DAVID UNDERSTOOD THE NEW TESTAMENT TRUTH THAT WE ARE TO OFFER TO GOD THE SACRIFICE OF PRAISE, NOT OF ANIMALS.

"By him therefore let us offer the sacrifice of praise to God continually, that is, the fruit of our lips giving thanks to his name" (Hebrews 13:15).

Those who see a return to the worship of the Psalms as a return to Old Testament Levitical law have missed the point entirely. David actually had a
"New Testament" understanding of praise and worship a thousand years early! Passages such as the following are certainly not "Old Testament" in theology at all, but teach "New Testament" truth:

Psalm 50:9,13,14 (NASB): *"I shall take no young bull out of your house, nor male goats out of your folds...Shall I eat the flesh of bulls, or drink the blood of male goats? Offer to God a sacrifice of THANKSGIVING..."*

Psalm 51:16,15 (NIV): *"You do not delight in sacrifice* (of animals), *or I would bring it; you do not take pleasure in burnt offerings...O Lord, open my lips and my mouth will declare your praise."*

4. GOD REJECTED THE TABERNACLE OF MOSES AND PLACED HIS PROPHETIC PRESENCE AND GLORY ON THE TABERNACLE OF DAVID IN ZION.

The Tabernacle of Moses was placed in Shiloh in the territory of Ephraim after Joshua conquered Canaan. Sometime between the death of Eli and the reign of David it was moved to Gibeon, north of Jerusalem. In David's day there were actually *two* tabernacles with two types of worship services operating at the same time. One was ritualistic and symbolic, the Tabernacle of Moses and the other, the Tabernacle of David in Zion, was filled with prophetic songs ("gifts of the Spirit") and the manifest presence of God. God rejected the Mosaic order of "worship" and chose instead the Davidic:

Psalm 78:60,68 (NIV): *"He* (God) *abandoned the tabernacle of Shiloh* (Moses'), *the tent he had set up among men...but he chose the tribe of Judah, Mount Zion* (site of David's Tabernacle) *which he LOVED."*

Psalm 87:1,2 (NIV): *"He has set his foundation on the holy mountain* (Zion); *the Lord LOVES the gates of Zion more than all the dwellings* (tabernacles) *of Jacob."*

Why did the Lord love David's Tabernacle in Zion? Because the praise and worship ordained by David around the ark manifested the same atmosphere of worship found in heaven! Zion was the earthly expression of the heavenly worship in which God continually dwells. God therefore "inhabited" the praises of earthly Zion just as He dwells in the worship of the heavenlies. His will was being "done in earth as it is in heaven."

Psalm 22:3: *"For thou art holy, O thou that inhabitest the praises of Israel."*

Psalm 132:13,14 (KJV, NIV): *"For the Lord hath chosen Zion; he hath desired it for his habitation. This is my resting place FOREVER and EVER; here will I sit enthroned..."*

5. ZION IS GOD'S DWELLING PLACE "FOREVER;" THE CHURCH, GOD'S DWELLING PLACE TODAY, IS THEREFORE AN EXPRESSION OF ZION.

The *church* is told in Hebrews 12:22,23 (NIV): *"You have*

come to MOUNT ZION...to the church of the firstborn..." Speaking of the foundation of the *church*, the apostles declared that Jesus was the chief cornerstone laid in *Zion* (see Romans 9:33; I Peter 2:4-8). The blood of the New Covenant is also associated with Zion: *"You have come to Mount Zion...to Jesus the mediator of a new covenant and to the sprinkled blood..."* (Hebrews 12:22,24 NIV). David prophesied concerning Calvary (Psalm 22) and the church received its regenerative work!

6. THE TABERNACLE OF DAVID IN ZION AND THE NEW TESTAMENT CHURCH ARE THEREFORE EXPRESSIONS OF THE SAME REALITY.

Jesus declared, *"I am the ROOT and the OFFSPRING of David..."* (Revelation 22:16). Jesus was the root of everything that grew in David's ministry: his worship and praise, his victorious warfare, his dominion and kingdom. Everything David was came originally from Jesus. And since Jesus is the source of everything in the church as well, then both David and the church have the same root: Jesus Christ. The same root produces the same fruit! Therefore the church is to manifest the same worship and praise, the same victory in warfare and the same kingdom and dominion as occurred in the life of David.

Jesus is also the "Offspring," or the "Son of David" (see Matthew 21:9). Peter preached on the day of Pentecost that Jesus had been raised from the dead to reign forever on David's throne (see Acts 2:25-31; compare Psalm 16:8-11). The throne of David originated in earthly Zion when David conquered all his enemies and exercised his authority over all the surrounding kingdoms of his day. Through the reigning King of Kings, Jesus Christ Who is sitting on the throne of David and exercising His authority over all principalities and powers, the church now operates as the extension of David's kingdom over all the nations of the earth. Isaiah prophesied of this universal reign of the Messiah and linked His kingdom rule to the restored Tabernacle of Davidas the extension of David's: *"In mercy shall the throne be established: and he* (the Messiah) *shall sit upon it in truth in the tabernacle of David, judging and seeking judgment and hasting righteousness"* (Isaiah 16:5).

7. THE EARLY CHURCH UNDERSTOOD ITSELF TO BE THE RESTORED TABERNACLE OF DAVID.

In every Old Testament revival after the days of David, when the presence of the Lord was restored to Judah, Davidic worship was restored also. For instance, in the days of the great revival under Hezekiah *"he set the Levites in the house of the Lord with cymbals, with psalteries and with harps, according to the commandment of David and of Gad the king's seer and Nathan the prophet; for so was the COMMANDMENT OF THE LORD BY HIS PROPHETS. And the Levites stood with the instruments of David...And all the congregation worshipped and the singers sang..."* (II Chronicles 29:25-30).

The Lord actually commanded the institution of Davidic worship through His prophetic word, for He loved the praise and worship of Zion! It is no surprise, then, to find the prophet Amos lifting his vision toward the church age and declaring that God would establish Zion again "in that day": *"In that day will I raise up the tabernacle of David that is fallen and close up the breaches thereof; and I will raise up his ruins and I will build it as in the days of old"* (Amos 9:11).

James quoted this prophecy from Amos and applied it directly to the church of his day, establishing the fact that he believed the church of Jesus Christ to be the restored Tabernacle of David! (See Acts 15:13-17).

8. THE EARLY CHURCH, AS THE EXPRESSION OF THE TABERNACLE OF DAVID, HAD A POWERFUL EVANGELISTIC IMPACT UPON THE GENTILES.

James quoted the prophet Amos to prove that it was the prophesied will of God for the Gentiles to become part of the Christian church, for the purpose of the restoration of the

Tabernacle of David was essentially evangelistic! *"That the residue of men might seek after the Lord and all the Gentiles..."* (Acts 15:17; see also Amos 9:12).

Here we see another reason why David was really more "New Testament" than "Old." He had a missionary spirit! What a refreshingly different attitude David had compared to the legalistic religious traditionalists of the Old Testament. He sang and prophesied extensively about all nations of the earth coming before the Lord in praise and worship:

Psalm 86:9: *"All nations whom thou hast made shall come and worship before thee, O Lord..."*

Psalm 117:1: *"O praise the Lord, all ye nations: praise him, all ye people."*

Psalm 72:11,17: *"Yea, all kings shall fall down before him: all nations shall serve him...all nations shall call him blessed."*

This missionary vision of David is still being fulfilled in our day as the Gospel of the kingdom is going to all the nations of the world and believers from "every kindred, tribe and tongue" are worshipping the Lord Jesus Christ according to the Psalms.

9. DAVIDIC WORSHIP WAS FILLED WITH GIFTS OF THE HOLY SPIRIT, ESPECIALLY PROPHECY.

The Psalms is the most prophetic book in the Old Testament, quoted more times both directly and indirectly in the New Testament than any other book. The Spirit of the Lord moved upon the singers and musicians in the worship services of the Tabernacle of David in Zion and they "prophesied." The sons of David's three main worship leaders, Asaph, Heman and Jeduthun, were ordained to *"prophesy with harps, with psalteries and with cymbals";* they *"prophesied according to the order of the king"* (I Chronicles 25:1-6).

In Davidic worship the Spirit of the Lord sang through the musicians and singers even as the prophetic Spirit of God moved in the early New Testament church. No wonder we find the apostle Paul referring to worship and praise as the means

15

of being filled with the Holy Spirit and the word of Christ!

Ephesians 5:18,19: *"Be filled with the Spirit;* (How?) *speaking to yourselves in psalms and hymns and spiritual songs, singing and making melody in your heart to the Lord."*

Colossians 3:16: *"Let the word of Christ dwell in you richly in all wisdom; teaching and admonishing one another* (in seminars, sermons and classes?) *in psalms and hymns and spiritual songs* ("songs of the Spirit")... "

The worship services of the Tabernacle of David, as well as those of the early New Testament church, were marked by an OPENNESS TO THE SPONTANEOUS MANIFESTATION OF SPIRITUAL GIFTS, allowing the prophetic Spirit of God to sing or speak through the worshippers. Hence the emphasis in the Psalms on the "new" songs we are to sing: *"He hath put a NEW song in my mouth..."* (Psalm 40:3; 33:3; 144:9). The early New Testament church was covered with such a prophetic atmosphere that unbelievers would be overcome with God's presence and start worshipping! *"But if all prophesy and there come in one that believeth not...the secrets of his heart* (are) *made manifest; and so falling down on his face, HE WILL WORSHIP GOD and report that God is in you of a truth"* (I Corinthians 14:24,25).

When Paul begins to enumerate the elements of the charismatic worship services in Corinth which were associated with such a strong prophetic presence of God, anointed songs were first on the list: *"when ye come together, every one of you hath a PSALM..."* (I Corinthians 14:26).

CONCLUSION

We have examined in detail the relationship between the church of Jesus Christ and the Tabernacle of David in Zion. In Zion the reality of God's presence was manifest in praise and worship and we have "come unto Mount Zion" in the church today! New Testament writers taught that Jesus Christ is the true Cornerstone in Zion, the church and Jesus described Himself as the "Root and Offspring of David." The apostles saw the church as the restored Tabernacle of David and as the extension of David's throne and kingdom on the earth. The same missionary vision for the nations was experienced in both the New Testament church and in the Tabernacle of David. Finally, the same prophetic presence of God was manifest in both the days of David and in the times of the New Testament, as new songs and prophetic revelation was poured out both in Old Testament Zion and in New Testament Zion, the church.

It is no wonder that "Davidic worship" is being restored today in the church of Jesus Christ worldwide and that churches everywhere are embracing the gloriously expressive worship of the Psalms. *The Lord loveth the gates of Zion more than all the dwellings of Jacob"* (Psalm 87:2).

3

WORSHIP — ARE WE MAKING ANY MISTAKES?
by Ernest Gentile

It happened on the Lord's day: John was "in the Spirit"! Suddenly the voice of God came like a trumpet (meaning it came from a long distance with a clear, distinct sound that cut through the distance).

The voice said to John, *"Come up here..."* (Revelation 4:1, NKJV*). John responded and was transported by the power of the Spirit. Spiritually he was caught up into the very presence of God. (I believe he was physically in a trance-like state. I don't think his body literally went to Heaven.)

The first thing that arrested his attention was the throne of God. Immediately he became aware of a Presence — and an atmosphere — that was different from anything he had ever experienced.

You know, of course, that everything has its environment of life. Fish live in the atmosphere of water and man in an

19

atmosphere of air. God lives in the environment of praise and worship. Just as the fish is most comfortable in the ocean and man is most comfortable surrounded by air, so God has chosen that His own life be maintained in an atmosphere of praise and worship. Constantly surrounding the throne of God are living creatures, angelic hosts and the people who have been redeemed from the earth; they all join in continually producing an atmosphere of jubilant glorification of God. That is the atmosphere in which John found himself.

JOHN'S MISTAKE

Of all the apostles I don't think you could find a man with a more worshipful heart than John. It was John who leaned his head against Jesus' bosom at the last supper. Yet an astounding thing is recorded about John in the book of Revelation.

It happened not just once, but twice, in the nineteenth and twenty-second chapters. John, in the excitement and power of the atmosphere of Heaven, fell down to worship an angel. *Can you imagine being in that heavenly atmosphere of great worship, yet making a mistake in whom you worship?* That's hard to believe! How could John, of all people, make such a mistake?

It is interesting that it happens towards the end of Revelation. Chapter 19 contains that memorable, tremendous thunder of praise. Repeatedly we read in that chapter "Hallelujah!" (which means "Praise ye the Lord") and "Praise our God." These are commands.

John is commanded to "Worship God!" when he begins to worship the angel (Revelation 19:10). Nevertheless, "Worship God!" had to be repeated in chapter 22:9 when John made his mistake a second time.

I would like to humbly suggest that if John could make such a mistake in heaven, we may be making a few mistakes in our worship services too. Would you agree? It is hard to be told that one is not worshipping properly. Nobody likes to hear that;

however, the Spirit of God wants to adjust us so that He can break into our churches in all His fullness.

EXCHANGING THE LIFEFLOW OF GOD

In Heaven, the living creatures are living by resurrection power. Such life is perpetual motion — once you have it you never die! With resurrection power you just keep moving in God. The very worship and praise of Heaven is perpetual motion in the sense that the holiness of God is continuously extolled. And the arrangement is reciprocal — that is, the praise of God's people is in response to the love of God that is moving out in waves of glory to the people of God. It is God and His people perpetually exchanging the lifeflow of God.

When we get to Heaven it will be so different from that to which we are accustomed. In fact, the nature of things in Heaven will be of such prophetic excellence that we will be able to instantly understand one another and even the very thinking of God.

In the church on earth, things should be somewhat the same. Whenever we Christians gather together and worship God there also should be that exchange of the lifeflow of God and a release of the gifts of the Spirit. Why is it that this is seldom seen in ordinary church services and functions? Could it be that the hearts of the people are centered more on function than on the Lord?

Ordinances and sacraments are certainly Scriptural, but many times God cannot be accommodated by our program or liturgy! In a lot of churches there is no room for the Lord. When He was born there was no room for Him in the inn and He still has that problem. He simply does not have opportunity to move in a free-flowing way among His people, because everything is so structured. If He came in wearing His royal regalia with a golden crown on His head we would pay more notice, but Christ is invisible and wants our worship to be "in spirit" (see John 4:24).

True worship focuses our minds so that God becomes the center of our attention. We are lifted out of ourselves, our spirits are released in God and He is released in us so that there is a flow of the spirits of the people to God and a flow of the Spirit of God back to His people. We give to God and He gives back to us. In Heaven this is taking place in the most excellent way. And so we desire to see God's will done, in the area of worship, on earth even as it is done in Heaven. Hallelujah!

A key text, Psalm 22:3, speaks of our holy God *"who inhabits* (or, who is enthroned upon) *the praises of Israel."* As we fill the atmosphere with our praise and worship of the Lord, our adoration literally creates a throne whereupon the Lord is pleased to dwell. Hebrews 2:12 (quoting from Psalm 22) tells us that the Son of God comes and sings in the midst of the church. Yes! The King comes amongst us as we worship Him. The King of the Church comes and sits upon the throne making His declarations and powerful statements (ex cathedra). Healings and charismatic manifestations then become evident because *we have made room for the Lord to work.*

It seems that the only thing God needs and seeks is worshippers. He could command us; He could cause earthquakes, fire and violence until we trembled on the ground, just as He did when the Ten Commandments were given. Instead He has chosen to wait for us to release our wills to enthrone Him in our worship.

Most Christians are trained in the ways of service: do this, do that. Those things are all important in their place, but if we are not careful we become Marthas and lose the heart of Mary. We must have, with all our formality, true hearts and spiritual vitality, worshipping in the Spirit. Unless you are pouring out your heart, all you are doing is mechanical and a far cry from the heavenly standard that John saw.

THE PSALMS MISTAKE

One worship mistake that is commonly made is the way in which the book of Psalms is handled. Many people associate Sunday morning worship and the reading of the Psalms. In our churches we read, for instance, *"Oh clap your hands, all you peoples! Shout to God with the voice of triumph"* (Psalm 47:1). But do we do what it says?

Even as a young person I wondered why, in the churches I attended, we *would read these statements yet never do them!* That question is still unanswered.

Every character and book of the Bible has a unique contribution to make to our fund of inspired knowledge. If we want to understand faith I would suggest we study Abraham. If you want to understand true meekness, study the life of Moses. If it's "justification by faith," read Romans. For proper church order, study I Corinthians. And when it comes to worship, there is no book (other than the book of Revelation, perhaps) that gives a better explanation than the book of Psalms.

David, "the sweet psalmist of Israel" (II Samuel 23:1), was a man after God's own heart (see Acts 13:22). This indicates that emotionally he was specially gifted by God to be open, receptive and flexible. Even though he committed the blackest sins of the Bible — murder and adultery (with Bathsheba) —his extraordinary heart is seen nonetheless, in that he went into such abject repentance that God took away his sin and blessed David's relationship with Bathsheba. Solomon, the next king of Israel was born from that union (see II Samuel 12:13,24). And furthermore, Jesus is known as the "Son of David." David's response to God was so thorough that he was blessed with sons who were the wisest men who ever lived.

David had a unique personality, a unique attitude and a unique heart after God. Because of this he was also gifted with unique insight concerning worship -- insight which was expressed in the book of Psalms. The Psalms were not meant to

23

be merely read, as is the case in most churches. Why do we read them? It is apparent that the very words have special significance when it comes to the adoration of God. They are inspiring and instructive words, but the tragedy is that we do not do what the words tell us to do. If God is telling us in His Word to do certain things, then let's do them!

Some ask me, do I not realize that such worship belongs to the Old Testament, 1000 years before Christ? And, therefore, should New Testament Christians follow that line of teaching?

I am saying that anything given in the Old Testament is appropriate for the New Testament Christian unless the New Testament says otherwise.

I will illustrate that for you. In the Old Testament God's people were not to eat certain foods, but in the New Testament we find that we are no longer under that obligation. You can eat anything you want if you do it with a grateful heart, unless it is something offered to idols (see Acts 16:29 and I Corinthians 8).

There are many things in the Old Testament that stop at the Cross. There are also, however, things that continue right on through the New Testament to the book of Revelation. Prayer, for instance, is something that didn't stop at the Cross. If anything Jesus intensified prayer. And we see that prayer goes all the way through the Bible.

Worship in the Bible progresses as the people of God move into new dimensions of understanding, until by the time you come to the book of Revelation, what was formerly a little stream has become a gushing river of thunderous praise to God. The heavens reverberate with the glory and power of the worship of almighty God.

In I Chronicles 28 we find David explaining how God gave him the plan of worship structure. Notice verses 11-13. *"David gave his son Solomon...THE PLANS FOR ALL THAT HE HAD BY THE SPIRIT...for the division of the priests and the Levites*

and for all the work of the service of the house of the Lord..."
This is significant. This is a prophetic revelation from God.
" 'All this,' said David, 'THE LORD MADE ME UNDERSTAND IN WRITING, BY HIS HAND UPON ME, ALL THE WORKS OF THESE PLANS' " (v. 19).

This revelation was not just for a little shepherd lad, but for all God's people, to make known to them that He wanted to dwell in an atmosphere of the adoration of God.

NEW TESTAMENT DAVIDIC WORSHIP

Today we approach the close of the ages and the significance of all Revelation portends, yet some people say, "We can't worship like that." Let us settle one very important question. Does the New Testament teach Davidic worship?

In Davidic worship we release our natural expressions and have them quickened by God. The book of Psalms and other Scriptures about David outline three main ways of doing this:
(1) with your mouth (singing, praising and shouting),
(2) with your hands (lifting, clapping and playing musical instruments) and
(3) with your body (bowing, standing and dancing).

Of course, you can do all these and still be very spiritually cold, but nevertheless, these are the basic ways of truly worshipping the Lord given in God's Word.

David's revelation was perpetuated by Solomon and wherever they had revival in ancient Israel they enjoyed and practised the principles of the Psalms. As we go into the New Testament we find that the New Testament writers did not shut off the true expression of worship. Some people think that the New Testament churches were as most churches are today. That is not true. There was a remarkable vitality in the early church.

Do we find the Davidic forms in the New Testament? In many Bible schools the New Testament is divided into five

25

sections: the Gospels, the book of Acts, the Pauline Epistles, the General Epistles and the book of Revelation. What I would like to do here is take examples from each of those sections to prove to you that the Davidic style of worship is to be in operation in the New Testament church.

First we will look at the Gospels. *"And suddenly there was with the angel a multitude of the heavenly host PRAISING God and saying: 'Glory to God in the highest and on earth peace, good will toward men!'"* (Luke 2:13,14) *"Then the shepherds returned, GLORIFYING and PRAISING God for all the things that they had heard and seen..."* (v. 20). The shepherds got excited and praised and glorified God with their mouths!

"They WORSHIPPED Him and returned to Jerusalem with great joy and were continually in the temple PRAISING and BLESSING God. Amen" (Luke 24:52-53). Were they whispering, do you suppose? No. They were praising God! Note Matthew 21:8ff, where the people shouted out praise to God (v.9) and where the children came into the temple making a noise, *"CRYING OUT...'Hosanna to the son of David'..."* (v.15). It says the chief priests and scribes *"were indignant"* (v.15), but Jesus said, *"Out of the MOUTH of babes and nursing infants you have perfected praise."* That, by the way, is a quotation from the Psalms. If you take the book of Psalms out of the New Testament you will find vacant spaces everywhere!

Next, Luke 6:23: *"Rejoice in that day* (the day of negatives and persecution) *and LEAP for joy!"* I think that means worshipping with your body, don't you?

Now Acts: *"...PRAISING God and having favour with all the people"* (Acts 2:47); *"...WALKING, LEAPING and PRAISING God"* (Acts 3:8); *"Paul and Silas were PRAYING and SINGING hymns to God and the prisoners were listening to them"* (Acts 16:25); *"I WORSHIP the God of my fathers..."* (Acts 24:14).

Now we will turn to the Pauline Epistles: *"...that the Gentiles might GLORIFY God for His mercy, as it is written: 'For this* reason I will CONFESS to You among the Gentiles and SING to Your name' And again he says: 'REJOICE, O Gentiles, with his people!' And again: 'PRAISE the Lord, all you Gentiles! LAUD Him, all you peoples!' " (Romans 15:9-11) All of this sounds like Davidic worship to me. Note here that Paul quotes from Deuteronomy 32, where the Hebrew word for "REJOICE" means "TO SPRING WITH HAPPINESS" — DANCING!

In the General Epistles we have Hebrews 13:15: *"By Him (Jesus) let us continually offer the sacrifice of praise to God, that is, THE FRUIT OF OUR LIPS, giving thanks to His name."*

Turning to the last section, the book of Revelation, we again see all three of the basic modes of expression. I must say that I wish Bible teachers would get more out of the book of Revelation than who the Antichrist is and when the time of the Tribulation will be. The worship in that book seems to be almost totally ignored.

In Revelation 19:1 we read: *"I heard a LOUD VOICE of a great multitude in heaven, saying, 'Alleluia! Salvation and glory and honor and power to the Lord our God!'"* "A loud voice" indicates vitality! God wants our strength. If we give Him our mind and our whole being with all our strength, we are fulfilling the first and great commandment.

In Revelation 5:8, 14:2 and 15:2 we are told of harpists who use their hands to play their instruments in praise unto the Lord.

In verse 4 of chapter 19 we read that the twenty-four elders and four living creatures *"fell down* (that is, they used their bodies) *and worshipped God who sat on the throne, saying, 'Amen! Alleluia!'"* Verse 5 says, " *'Praise our God, all you His servants and those who fear him, both small and great!'* "

How are we going to glorify God? By following and obeying the Scriptural methods. Our praises must fulminate (make a loud, thunderous noise) across the land, as in Revelation, until our churches are echoing with the praising of God. Why?

Because when true praise gets a hold of people, *the Lord our God the Almighty reigns!*

GOD'S REVELATION

The church has every authority to employ and enjoy the Davidic style of worship, quickened by the Holy Spirit. We can worship as David did, but with a new impetus because we can have the power of the Holy Ghost working in us, quickening those truths in our hearts.

In our worship God is wanting us to know His power and be indwelt by the Holy Spirit. God wants our buildings to be filled with those who are worshipping God in the Spirit. When this happens we will discover that people are being converted in astounding ways.

In II Chronicles 9 we read of the Queen of Sheba's visit to Solomon. When she arrived she was amazed at the wisdom of Solomon, but the thing that really caught her breath away was the king's ascent (v. 4). I believe that what captured her attention was not his staircase or anything like that, but rather the king and the people of God going up to the temple of God.

What is going to characterize the church in the last days? I believe it will be the awe it produces among the unbelievers when they see us ascend in our worship according to the pattern revealed to David. So many people are going around burdened with overwhelming problems. They have tensions, marital discord and all the other things that are afflicting our generation. But now they are beginning to see God's people striding with strength into the house of the Lord. They hear a strange sound, a joyful sound and ask, "What have they got to praise God about?"

They will see us using our full faculties of expression under the quickening power of the Spirit and they will sense the presence of the Lord. With that presence will be prophetic wisdom and insight, the awareness of sin and sensitivity to the moving of God and His righteousness. The "Queens of Sheba" of the last days will see the moving of God and as predicted in I Corinthians 14:25 they will confess, *"God is truly among you..."*

*All Scripture quotations in this article are from the **New King James Version** of the Bible.

TEACHING &
ADMONISHING IN SONG
by Larry Dempsey

"**L**et the WORD OF CHRIST dwell in you richly in all wisdom; teaching and admonishing one another in psalms and hymns and spiritual songs; singing with grace in your hearts to the Lord" (Colossians 3:16).

What a revelation Paul gave us! Just think — we are to *teach* and *admonish* each other with worship! And what's more, it is to be done out of the deposit of the *WORD* that is in us. What a revelation! What a challenge! What a RESPONSI-BILITY! If I am to be a member of the body that supplies edifying admonishment by my example as a worshipper, then I must have the *WORD dwelling in me richly.*

THE INDWELLING WORD
The rich indwelling of the Word will cause you to have a *mature* worship vocabulary. Have you ever noticed the brand-new babes in Christ in the local assembly? They pick up on a

few standard "praise-phrases" such as "hallelujah, thank-you Jesus, glory to God" and during times of corporate worship this is all they know how to say! But watch them as they begin to read and study the Word. Their worship vocabulary increases service after service. It isn't long until their hands are lifted high and melodious praises are flowing from their mouths: "Hallelujah! You are Lord and the Glory and Lifter of my head; You are the King of Glory; You are the Governor among the nations..." What happened? The *WORD* began to dwell in them richly and their praise began to reflect the deposit of the Word in them. HALLELUJAH! Barry Griffing has a saying, *"WORD in...SONG out!"*

TEACHING AND ADMONISHING
ONE ANOTHER

We teach and admonish through singing of psalms, hymns and our spiritual songs (corporate singing of spontaneous praises and the prophetic Song of the Lord). Because of this "teaching factor" that is present in worship, we have often unintentionally taught wrong concepts of God, heaven, the Christian life and various points of major Bible doctrine.

For many years most "full-gospel" churches sang songs that primarily exalted heaven as the goal of the Christian, though Scripture plainly teaches that transformation into God's image and likeness is the goal of the Christian. Through our music we taught the believer to struggle and "hold on" down here until, at some point in the future, we would be instantly zapped to heaven in the rapture and all our troubles would be over! Then, in heaven, we'd dangle our feet in the crystal river, live in mansions with gates of pearl, float on clouds playing a harp all day, etc., etc. The music gave the general impression that the precious gift of eternal life consisted largely of a euphoric state of sublime laziness!

We extolled through song the important fact that "daddy

sang bass and mama sang tenor..." We pined and whined for "mansions over hilltops," and musically declared that our goal was to have a "cabin in the corner of gloryland." Generations of pentecostal youth grew up around that type of religious music, which fostered sentimental outbursts of weeping (often mistaken for moves of the Holy Spirit), or emotional releases that sometimes resulted in fleshly displays of screaming, violent quakings, uncontrolled bodily spasms and other manifestations which did little to contribute to the edification of the body as a whole.

I was raised in this type of church environment and these saints were sincere and honest in their activities (thank God for my Pentecostal heritage!), but we had little or no idea of what it meant to *bring* the sacrifice of praise into the house of the Lord and to *offer* to God our bodies as living sacrifices of spiritual worship. Our concept was that nothing could be done, no one could move, dance, or rejoice unless the Spirit "hit" him. Consequently, we would be released in the realm of emotion only after repeated choruses of "Jesus on the Mainline, Tell Him What You Want" or some other similar soulish-oriented song. We *taught* that concept through singing songs that had very little Scriptural truth in them!

Is it any wonder the Bible is being sung again? The Spirit of God has moved in mighty power during the past few decades, so that the SCRIPTURES, especially the Psalms, are springing to life anew in the church. They are being sung as worship choruses, choral anthems — even entire musical productions based on Scripture. PRAISE GOD! *You can't receive any purer doctrine than the Word of God!* People are being taught sound doctrine because they are being taught and admonished with the MUSIC FROM GOD'S WORD!

The writers of those grand old hymns of the faith knew the importance of this! They penned "Crown Him With Many Crowns," "Amazing Grace," "O, For a Thousand Tongues To

Sing," "Glorious Things of Thee Are Spoken, Zion, City of Our God," "All Hail the Power of Jesus' Name," and scores of others. These *always-current* hymns teach *GOOD DOCTRINE.* The orthodox Christian faith flourished in sound doctrine until the arrival of dispensationalism in the 1800's. This *un*-orthodox doctrine then permeated the evangelical-fundamentalist branch of Christendom and the songs soon began to reflect the errors of this "futurist" theology. We became consumed with heaven, mansions, streets of gold, the rapture, flying away at any moment, etc. and the songs of power, majesty, dominion and glory were ignored.

But, HALLELUJAH!, these are days of revival and restoration and once again the Dominion Psalms are being sung, the majestic hymns are being heard and Zion is rejoicing again! The Lord's house is being established in the top of the mountain! We are dancing, rejoicing, prophesying on instruments, releasing the Song of the Lord and celebrating the glorious Presence of our King! We are learning the joyful principles of discipleship and letting the Holy Spirit form the heart of the servant in us.

These are *historic days!* In Acts 2:4 the Lord came "suddenly to his temple," the church (compare Malachi 3:1) and empowered us with power from on high. We are a dominion people! We are a people of prophetic purpose! Let us continue to praise and worship God in psalms, hymns and spiritual songs. Let us ascend Zion with high praise in our mouth, a two-edged sword in our hand and the dew of the latter rain upon our heads!

PART II

GOD'S PURPOSE
FOR PRAISE & WORSHIP

THE FULL PURPOSE
OF WORSHIP
by Bob Sorge

Have you ever asked the question, "Why do we spend so much time in our services on worship?" What is the reason for all the present emphasis on worship?

It is essential that every pastor and church answer this question for themselves. It is no longer adequate to defend our worship services by saying, "Well, we've always done it this way." It is equally insufficient to conceive of our worship services as "the preliminaries," something to "condition" the congregation in preparation for the truly important part of the service: the sermon. It is time to seriously consider from a broader perspective the vital role that worship plays in the life of the congregation.

There are three general spheres in which our worship services minister: 1. There is the *vertical* aspect of worship, the level in which the worshipper communicates with the Lord;

2. There is the *horizontal* aspect of worship, the level in which the worshipper communicates with others in the congregation;
3. There is the *inward* aspect of worship, where the worshipper is personally affected by the worship service. Each of these areas helps us to better understand the role of worship in the congregation.

THE VERTICAL ASPECT OF WORSHIP

The very first and primary reason for worship is to minister to the Lord. The basic posture of the worshipper is, "I will bless the Lord," not "Lord, bless me!" We all know this, but let us face it — there are times when we go home from a worship service and complain because the worship did not do as much for us as it did last week. If the main purpose for worship is to bless and glorify the Lord then why am I upset when it does not seem to bless me? The question should not be whether the worship service blessed me; the question is, did it bless God? It is not what I thought of the worship service that matters -- it is what God thought of it! Did *He* approve? Was *He* pleased with our "sacrifice of praise?" On us has been bestowed the unique and glorious honour of actually blessing the Lord God Almighty! We are the Levitical order of the New Testament, called by God to minister before Him (see I Peter 2:5,9). Let's take full advantage of this special privilege!

A second reason for our worship services is to realize the manifest presence of God in our midst. We understand that God is everywhere at all times, yet there are different degrees to which God manifests Himself. He manifests Himself on one level "where two or three are gathered." But when a larger group of God's people congregate to sing His glorious praise, He "inhabits" those praises and reveals His presence in a special way among His praising people. (See Psalm 22:3 and II Chronicles 5:13,14).

It was in Exodus 33 that the Lord made this special promise

to Moses: *"My Presence will go with you and I will give you rest"* (v. 14, NIV*). Moses' response was, *"If your Presence does not go with us, do not send us up from here... What else will distinguish me and your people from all the other people on the face of the earth?"* (vv. 15,16). The same goes for us today. What will distinguish us, as God's people, from the people of the world? What makes our church services different from the meetings of any other social or service organization? The presence of God! If we don't have God's presence in our services, we may as well dismiss and throw a picnic instead.

The presence of God is the earmark of the church. That is how sinners will know we are different! When they sense the presence of God in our midst they will have experienced the reality all men truly desire.

We also hold worship services in order to provide an opportunity for the power of God to be released in His church. In Luke 5:17 we are told that while Jesus was teaching *"the power of the Lord was present for him to heal the sick."* This tells us that in the presence of God the power of God is revealed. It is true that God maintains sovereign control over the working of His mighty power — we cannot coerce Him into demonstrating His power simply because we have worshipped. But when God's presence is manifest in the midst of the congregation, there comes an atmosphere that gives God greater freedom to work according to the counsel of His will. Worship prepares us to become ready recipients of the blessing of God.

We also worship in order to provide an atmosphere or seedbed for the gifts of the Spirit and various spiritual ministries to be manifested. Have you noticed that prophecies rarely come forth until *after* God's people have worshipped for a season? This is not accidental. First we worship, *then* spiritual

---

* All Scriptural quotations in this article are taken from the New International Version, unless otherwise noted.

37

ministries begin to operate. It is not that God is unwilling to speak prophetically to His people at the beginning of the service, but we are not often ready to flow in the gifts of the Spirit.

Finally, in this vertical sense of worship, we worship in order to open up the channels of communication between us and God. A number of people attending a Sunday service have not communicated with God since last Sunday! This is lamentable, but true. They may have not read their Bibles or spent quality time in prayer all week. The worship service provides them the opportunity to confess their sins, open up their hearts to the Lord and receive cleansing and renewal from Him. In the Song of Solomon the Lover begs of the beloved: *"Show me your face, let me hear your voice; for your voice is sweet and your face is lovely"* (2:14). This is the call of our Lord to His bride. Can you imagine the Lord, with great yearning and emotion in His voice, calling to His people many times in this fashion? This is the heartbeat of God for our worship services! He wants to see our face lifted up to Him. O, how He wants to hear our voice singing sweet praises to Him! The Lord so longs for His people to overcome their inhibitions in the congregation, that they might with open face and strong voice radiate His praise.

THE HORIZONTAL
ASPECT OF WORSHIP

The interpersonal dynamics of a worship service are more significant than many realize. Consider, first, that we worship in order to enhance the feelings of unity within a body of believers. Can you remember experiencing one of those altar services where most have gone home and a few have stayed behind to pray and worship? It is a time when the few folks who remain are worshipping the Lord with everything that is within them. You look over at the one next to you and realize that he is unabashedly pouring out his soul to the Lord. At that moment you feel a tremendous affinity with that brother because he, like you, is totally committed to the Lord. There is a tremendous sense of unity that comes over the group and soon everyone is hugging each other!

This bond is greater than the unity we feel simply as Christians in the body of Christ. This bond comes from the unity we feel as fellow-worshippers with hearts that seek after God. Show me a church that worships with all their heart, soul, mind and strength and I will show you a church that is moving ahead for God with an extraordinary sense of unity.

We also worship in order to provide believers with an opportunity to confess and profess their faith before others. We usually find it comparatively easy to confess the Lord in the congregation, during the worship service. But it's another thing altogether to confess the Lord to our unsaved neighbors, co-workers, friends and relations. But confessing the name of the Lord in the worship service increases our boldness and faith to declare His name before unbelievers. Lift your voice in the congregation — "lift it up, be not afraid" — and the Lord will increase your ability to vocalize your faith to others.

Another key reason for congregational worship is that we might declare the glories of God before unbelievers. The unsaved do visit our worship services and this is an excellent opportunity for them to see the reality of the glory of the Lord. Psalm 108:3 declares, *"I will praise you, O Lord, among the nations; I will sing of you among the peoples."* It is clearly God's intention that His praises not be confined to the ears of believers.

For too long God's people have been bashful about the praise of God! We sometimes think like this: "I'm not going to bring my neighbor to the Sunday evening service, because our church gets too carried away in worship and I don't want to turn my neighbor off." But a worship service is the best place to bring an unsaved friend; when God manifests His presence in the midst of His people, unbelievers will be apprehended by the convicting power of the Holy Spirit and drawn to the Lord. Do you want to win your neighbors for the Lord? Take them to the hottest praise service you can find! They don't need to understand what they see, they only need to experience the reality of our God. And we do not need to apologize for or explain the praises, we only need to declare His praises. God intends for His praise to be broadcast around the world! Let us look for the day when singing groups will set up in City Square and do nothing but sing praises to the Lord. Open up the windows of your church, lift up the shades, swing wide the doors and sing His praise before the world!

As a final consideration of the horizontal aspects of worship, we worship in our churches in order to create a proper mood for the sermon and the remainder of the service. It has been the experience of countless pastors that when the worship is real and vibrant it is definitely easier to preach. Not only is the anointing of the Spirit more evident, but the hearts of the people are more open to hear the Word of the Lord. There is a phrase in Hosea 10:11 which reads, *"Judah shall plow..."* (KJV). Judah means "praise," so therefore we might say that "praise plows." Praise plows the soil of our hearts so that we are prepared to have the seed of the Word of God implanted. It is not accidental that most churches flow in worship *prior* to the preaching of the Word.

THE INWARD ASPECT OF WORSHIP

Finally let us consider the ways in which worship changes the worshipper within. We conduct worship services in order to release each person into uninhibited expression of praise and worship. Many saints are introverted in their expression of worship, in much the same way as many husbands are reserved in their expressions of love toward their spouses. One of the clear goals of our worship services, therefore, is to see these introverted worshippers released in their expression of love and adoration to the Lord.

We recognize that all saints worship differently, according to the unique nature of their own personality, but it is pleasing to the Lord when we are totally liberated to worship Him according to our true nature. When someone is very inhibited in a worship service but very extroverted while watching a ball game, I am not convinced they are being true to their personality in the worship service! According to the Lord's prayer, we should strive for worship *"in earth, as it is in heaven"* (Matthew 6:10). The unique quality about worship in heaven is that it is totally free of any pride, inhibition, sophistication, or pompous dignity. Let us pray that the Lord will release us into *that* dimension of freedom even in this life.

Worship services also teach and reinforce spiritual truth. The apostle Paul stated it in this way: *"TEACHING and AD-MONISHING one another in psalms and hymns and spiritual songs..."* (Colossians 3:16, KJV). Because many of our choruses are taken from the Bible, we are actually memorizing the Scripture when we sing them. In this manner we and our children are learning the Word of God. Also, many of the hymns we sing are rich with theological and devotional meaning. It is safe to say that the songs we sing are teaching our children the practical theology of the church.

Our songs of worship also provide the worshipper with the means to express heart-felt attitudes that are otherwise difficult to express. Most of us are not poets, nor are many of us fluent speakers. Many Christians have difficulty putting into words the depths of love and emotion they feel toward the Lord. But in our hymnals we have recorded the words of men like Charles Wesley who were particularly gifted in expressing themselves with the pen. Thus we can echo the words of the hymn-writer, who has provided our feelings with a vocabulary of choice words and an enhancing melody. The song becomes a meaningful expression from my heart to the Lord.

Another very important reason for worship is to birth a heart for holiness in each individual. In this regard we learn an important principle from Psalm 115:4-8. That portion describes the false gods of the heathen, saying they can't see or smell. It adds that *"Those who make them will be like them..."* (v. 8). The principle is this: *We become like that which we worship.* Therefore, as we worship the Lord we are changed into His very likeness!

II Corinthians 3:18 is a beautiful verse describing this process: *"And we, who with unveiled faces all reflect the Lord's glory, are being transformed into his likeness with ever-increasing glory..."* When we worship with an uplifted countenance we truly reflect the Lord's glory. It is then that we are changed little by little, becoming more like the God we worship. "Worship doesn't change me," you might say. "I go out the same as when I came in to the church." If worship doesn't change your life, the reason is simple: You haven't unveiled your face before God! To unveil your face you must relinquish your inhibitions, your "charismatic sophistication," or whatever other hindrance may beset you and pour out your heart to the Lord with tears of repentance and contrition. *That* is true worship and that will change your life!

I John 3:2 gives us a tremendous promise: *"But we know that when he appears, we shall be like him, for we shall see him as he is."* Isaiah saw the Lord in worship, high and lifted up and he was never the same again. Daniel saw the Lord in worship and fell as one dead. The apostle John saw the Lord and fell prostrate in worship. You are promised that when *you* see the Lord in worship, *you shall be like Him!* If you will draw close to the all-holy God you will inevitably be changed.

Another clear purpose for worship is to inspire a life of worship in each believer. It is relatively easy to get excited about worship in the midst of the congregation, but too many operate at that level alone. They worship only when they feel inspired to do so. But God is not satisfied with merely spontaneous worship. The Lord is seeking those who will be worshippers seven days a week. You see, there is a difference between one who worships and a worshipper. It is not so much how enthusiastically you worship on Sunday that matters; it is how enthusiastic a worshipper you are on Monday! In I Chronicles 9:33 we read that the Levitical singers ministered before the Lord twenty-four hours a day. For us New Testament Levites, this is the pattern.

Some people wait for the worship leader to push their "worship button." If he doesn't lead out in the right song at the right time, they just will not enter in. Let us determine to follow God's Word, to stir ourselves to *continually* offer up the sacrifice of praise (see Hebrews 13:15). Worship in the congregation is practice time — out in the world we discover if we learned the lesson! Are we in fact becoming true worshippers? If so, it will be manifest in a life that is dedicated continually as a living sacrifice before the Lord.

PRAISE PREPARES

In conclusion, a final purpose for worship is that through worship God is preparing us for the new thing He is wanting to do. Luke 1:17 reads, *"to make ready a people prepared for the Lord."* God is preparing *people*; He is preparing you and me, the church of Jesus Christ. Once we are prepared to receive it, the Lord will surely send His new move. And praise prepares.

Psalm 50:23 in the NIV translation says, *"He who sacrifices thank offerings honors me and he PREPARES THE WAY so that I may show him the salvation of God."* Worship softens our hearts and sensitizes our spirit to the Spirit of God. Then, when the Spirit moves we are prepared to follow, no matter how unorthodox or unexpected the new way seems to be. We must be attuned to the gentle prompting of the Spirit in order to follow Him and worship fine-tunes our heart to the Lord. If we are accustomed to gazing steadily upon His face in worship, then when He moves we'll notice. May we be the kind of people whose hearts are so prepared through worship that we are ready to move with God!

With a clearer understanding of why we worship, our services will not drift aimlessly but will move forward incisively toward the goal set before us. Our goal? To be worshippers. Why? To minister to the Lord and to one another, to experience His glorious presence and to remain sensitized to His voice. This is the call of the Spirit to the church today. Are *you* hearing His voice?

6

MUSIC: IT'S ORIGIN, PURPOSES & POWER
by Mark Melby

"The Lord answered Job...and said...Where wast thou when I laid the foundations of the earth...when the morning stars sang together and all the sons of God shouted for joy?" (Job 38:1-7)

Here, in what most Biblical scholars believe to be the oldest book in the Bible, we see a beautiful picture of the angelic host singing and shouting as God was creating the universe. One can imagine that as it was being formed, music was being built into every part of creation.

The Word of God confirms this in numerous passages. We read of the mountains singing in Isaiah 44:23, the valleys and the hills singing and shouting in Psalm 65:13 and Psalm 98:8, the stones crying out in Luke 19:40 and the trees of the wood singing out at the presence of the Lord in I Chronicles 16:33 and Isaiah 44:23. On and on the accounts go, telling of the handiwork of the Lord singing, clapping, shouting and crying out to Him.

Picture in your mind's eye the precision, the perfect timing and the accuracy of God putting each thing in its place. As God spoke, there was! And it was just as He said it would be. There were no mistakes, no wrong notes being played as the entire universe moved together in one grand and glorious, harmonious symphony!

But this is not where it all begin, is it?

WHERE DID IT BEGIN?

We understand from the above quotation from the book of Job that the angelic host was created even before the universe was formed — and they were musical! In fact, Scripture gives us a very clear portrait of one angel in particular as being a virtual "one-man band" (if I may use that term for lack of a better one). Lucifer, one of the three angels named in Scripture (his name means "Day-star" or "Son of the Morning" — see Isaiah 14:12), was created perfect in beauty and full of wisdom (see Ezekiel 28:12). The workmanship of his tabrets and his pipes was prepared in him in the day he was created (see Ezekiel 28:13). Also, the sound of his viols is heard in Isaiah 14:11. In other words, in Lucifer were the three basic categories of musical instruments that we know today: the stringed instruments (represented by the "viols"), the wind instruments (represented by the "pipes") and the percussion instruments (represented by the "tabrets").

The wording of Ezekiel 28 indicates that Lucifer used his music ministry to lead all the angelic host in worship of God. He is called "the anointed cherub that covereth" (screens, protects), which indicates that he was guardian of the throne of God. However, iniquity was found in him (Ezekiel 28:15) and he was cast out of heaven with approximately one third of the angels (see Jude 6; II Peter 2:4; Matthew 25:41). Nevertheless, he did not forfeit his musical abilities, nor did God take away this ministry from him. *"The gifts and callings of God are without repentance"* (Romans 11:29). Today, Satan is using music as a tool against God and the church.

From studying these and other portions of Scripture, there can be no doubt as to the origin of music. From the very heart of the Divine Creator, music was put into most everything He touched!

WHY HAS GOD ORDAINED IT?

As we look through the Scriptures, we see hundreds of references to music, singing, playing of instruments, etc. God obviously is saying something to us about the importance and purpose of it.

Singing is as old as humanity itself. It plays a part in every aspect of living, from the deeply religious rituals of the various civilizations, to the shouting, singing and playing of instruments in warfare, to the ordinary, everyday, cultural work life. Even today, in our society, we witness music in every aspect of our daily living. We can't walk into a department store nor listen to a commercial on television or radio without hearing music of some kind or another. Why does music fill our lives so, permeating to the very core of our existence?

Besides putting music into the things He created, God also put something into the heart of every man He created — the desire to respond to music. And respond man does! Even the person who says he "can't carry a tune in a bucket" finds himself tapping his foot to a snappy rhythm he hears. Man is most vulnerable when it comes to music. The meanest, hardest heart melts like butter when played the right song and the meek, timid person can be stirred to defend his country by singing the right song. This response factor Divinely created in the very being of man is evidence that God has definite purposes for music in our lives.

But there is more direct evidence. God *commands* that music be used in our lives. Psalm 81:1-3 is not a suggestion from the Lord, but a dictate that we are to *"sing aloud unto God our strength: make a joyful noise unto the God of Jacob. Take a psalm and bring hither the timbrel, the pleasant harp with the psaltery. Blow up the trumpet in the new moon, in the time appointed, on our solemn feast day."* We, as worshippers of God, are to be excited and stir up both ourselves and others to give unto the Lord the glory due His name. Music is to be used to express our delight in the Lord and to communicate that delight, first to God in praise and worship and then to others. Any other use of music, if it is not first used to worship and exalt the Lord Jesus Christ, is below the purpose for which God has ordained it.

GOD'S PURPOSES FOR MUSIC

God commands the use of music in three main areas of our lives: in worship, in teaching and in evangelism.

The highest ministry of music is to the Lord in worship and praise. As ministering priests we are to offer spiritual sacrifices that are pleasing and acceptable to God (see Hebrews 13:15). We are to love, admire and reverence Him. God did not create music to cause us to center our affections on the one who is playing or singing the music; He created it to be a way of channeling our affections to Him. Psalm 95:1-2 says, *"O come, let us sing unto the Lord: let us make a joyful noise to the rock of our salvation. Let us come before his presence with thanksgiving and make a joyful noise unto him with psalms."* We must be careful to sing "unto the Lord," and in our service of song to take care that all we offer is with a sincere heart and fervent intent directed towards the Lord Jesus Himself!

Second, another of God's purposes for music is teaching. A familiar portion of Scripture, Colossians 3:16, says, *"Let the word of Christ dwell in you richly in all wisdom; teaching and admonishing one another in psalms and hymns and spiritual songs, singing with grace in your hearts to the Lord."* Here we clearly see that even in teaching with psalms, hymns and spiritual songs, it is to be done with grace in our hearts to the Lord! By teaching the Word of God in song, we take those who are born again from the position of merely knowing Jesus Christ as Saviour, into the place of spiritual maturity.

Third, music can be used as a powerful instrument in reaching the unsaved. Sometimes, when just words would not speak to someone, a song has the ability to open the resistant heart and turn that person toward the Lord.

Of course I realize that much more could be said about God's purposes for music — the above is only a brief outline. Most important of all, we need to understand that our music must be exercised under the guidance and power of the Holy Spirit, so that it will penetrate through to our spirits, causing us to come alive to God!

THE POWER OF MUSIC

"Then an herald cried aloud, To you it is commanded, O people, nations and languages, that at what time ye hear the sound of the cornet, flute, harp, sackbut, psaltery, dulcimer and all kinds of musick, ye fall down and worship the golden image that Nebuchadnezzar the king hath set up: and whoso falleth not down and worshippeth shall the same hour be cast into the midst of a burning fiery furnace" (Daniel 3:4-6).

This is an example of the power of music used negatively. At the sound of the music all the people, no matter where they were from nor who they had worshipped before, were to fall down and worship King Nebuchadnezzar. And for those who wouldn't fall down, a fiery furnace awaited. Here, music — the playing of instruments — was used as a powerful tool to soften the minds of those who were foolish enough to yield, bringing them into compliance with the king's command. Amid all the mirth and gaiety of the music, they would cast down their affections to a false god.

God wants to use music positively, to cause us to cast our affections at His feet. Over and over the Word exhorts us to *"worship the Lord in the beauty of holiness"* (I Chronicles 16:29; II Chronicles 20:21; Psalm 29:2; 96:9; etc.). Our music, our worship, is to be directed only toward the Lord, to the Person of Jesus Christ.

The power of music used rightly is shown in II Chronicles 5:13-14, where it is recorded that *"it came even to pass, as the trumpeters and singers were as one, to make one sound to be heard in praising and thanking the Lord; and when they lifted up their voice with the trumpets and cymbals and instruments of musick and praised the Lord, saying, For he is good; for his mercy endureth for ever: that then the house was filled with a cloud, even the house of the Lord; so that the priests could not stand to minister by reason of the cloud: for the glory of the Lord had filled the house of God."*

It was not when the singers and musicians offered sacrifices, but when they sang and played, that God gave them favor. When they praised God, the house was filled with a cloud. It was a simple song they sang, yet the result was that the priests could not stand to minister for the very glory and presence of the Lord descended upon them. Powerful, anointed music draws people into the presence of the Lord and causes them to cast their affections to Him.

We must not come to church just to be entertained. We must open our minds and our spirits to God. The anointing of the Lord is essential, not just upon the musicians, but also upon the congregation. If our music isn't touching our spirits, then we are not tapping its power to accomplish the purposes that God intends for it!

POWER TO PREPARE

There are many other areas that could be discussed more extensively as to the purposes and power of music. For instance, music promotes unity. When we sing and worship, conflicting moods disappear and people are drawn together to harmonize in unity. *"Thy watchmen shall lift up the voice; with the voice together shall they sing: for they shall see eye to eye, when the Lord shall bring again Zion. Break forth into joy, sing together, ye waste places of Jerusalem: for the Lord hath comforted his people, he hath redeemed Jerusalem"* (Isaiah 52:8,9).

Music originated with God and is ordained by God to help accomplish His purposes — the restoration of lives, families, churches and nations. Ultimately, it serves to prepare His universal church, the Bride of the Lamb, for the glorious return of the Bridegroom, Jesus Christ.

"And I heard as it were the voice of a great multitude and as the voice of many waters and as the voice of mighty thunderings, saying, Alleluia: for the Lord God omnipotent reigneth. Let us be glad and rejoice and give honour to him: for the marriage of the Lamb is come and his wife hath made herself ready" (Revelation 19:6-7).

7

MUSIC'S POWER
IN THE HOME
by Andrew Picklyk

Have you ever noticed how the world of business, advertising and entertainment has capitalized on and exploited the power of music? It is common knowledge that music produces responses in people and can therefore be used to create desired results in the world of buying and selling. Movies are a prime example. Specially orchestrated movie music is used to produce a whole range of audience responses.

Music has the ability to communicate and influence. It has the power to transmit thoughts and emotions in such a way that the listener readily picks them up. It is like a vehicle that carries freight. Vehicles can carry all kinds of products, good or bad, constructive or destructive. With music, thoughts and emotions are the freight and music is the carrier.

The Bible says that while men slept, the enemy came and

53

deposited harmful elements among the good (see Matthew 13:24-30). Today, much effort and many dollars are expended to provide health and wholesomeness for our families. Yet all too often the vehicle of music comes right into our living room and drops off loads of untested, often poisonous freight. We ought to realize now what is being unloaded, because the time will come when it will be very evident (v. 26).

The power of music — for good or evil — must not be underestimated. It affects our entire being, reaching through the physical right into our soul and even into the spirit realm. Depending on the nature of the music, it can and will very quickly either lift up our spirits or influence us in some other way. We can use it to bless God, ourselves and others, or we can allow it to be used to harm us and our families.

God created music as the channel for communion with Him. He wants us to approach Him with singing (see Psalm 100:2). Heaven, the place where music originated, is filled with glorious musical sounds. The Bible says it sounds like the sound of many waters (see Revelation 1:15). Music is part of the nature of God Himself; it rightfully belongs to Him and His kingdom.

Because God wants to commune with us through music, He designed us with a built-in desire for it. Throughout Scripture, God's people used music to express themselves to Him, as in their celebrations of great accomplishments. But man's built-in desire for music is also evidenced in many natural ways, not all of them good. Our world is truly a world of music. The tons of music technology that are sold and used today are astounding. Dispensers of music come in all shapes and sizes. Music is available at our fingertips and few commodities are more affordable. Of course, not all of the music in the world is evil in itself, but what music is used for and what it communicates should be questioned.

The problem is that Satan, too, is very aware of the power

of music. It is believed that before Lucifer's fall he was responsible for music in heaven (see Ezekiel 28:11-19; Isaiah 14:4-
20). He became proud, however — arrogant, self-willed and
rebellious against God. He brought discord, conflict, division
and eventually death. Hell is now his headquarters, the world
and humanity his challenge. He is endeavouring to advance his
rule of deception and he wields a master weapon — music!

Since Satan is asserting himself against the will of God,
everything he does is against the principles of life. He is a
promoter of death and evil, so everything sourced in him produces the same. The devil cannot sing God's music because it
is contrary to the intention of his evil kingdom. His music has
to be, then, of a nature that will identify and inspire the works
of darkness and evil.

Look at the effect of some of the wrong music of our day:
mass hysteria, violence and people being stampeded to death
are some of its excesses. Sin, immorality and rebellion are all
too often the content of the productions. Principles of Godliness
are undermined by the lyrics, which are no longer hard to
understand or just suggestive, but are clearly communicating
their sins and filth. The hearers become totally captivated and
addicted to this idolatry of our day.

Such music corrupts wholesome values and degenerates
society, yet the evil communicators who produce it have become the stars and heroes of our day. Their products are available anywhere. Society is in increasing turmoil, yet this turmoil
is subtly supported and promoted by what is labelled entertainment.

Answer these questions honestly to yourself, before God.
They will help you to qualify your music.

1. What is produced by the music I listen to? Jesus said, *"By
their fruits ye shall know them"* (Matthew 7:20). Good music
develops the Christ-like character and produces joy and

harmony in life and relationships. If music caters to the sin nature of lusts and fleshly desires, it will debase the quality of life.

2. What kind of activities accompanies my music? What places is it comfortable in? Does it require a sin atmosphere or one of righteousness?

3. Who performs and uses this music? What is the life-style of the people who enjoy this kind of music? There is an old insight that says, "Birds of a feather flock together." Music is known by who produces and identifies with it. It is important to consider the producer's intent or purpose for the music, remembering that we transmit what we are. Values or the lack of them are communicated through the medium of music by its producers.

4. Does this music glorify God? Is it used to promote His ways? The best music promotes worship and communication with God and creates a hunger for the things of God. Since He is the Originator of truly good music, He ought to have the final say concerning it.

When you have honestly considered these questions, go through your collection of music. Check it out carefully. When God gives you guidance by His Holy Spirit, respond and take action. Save your family and others around you from negative music influences. Your reward will be the blessing of the Lord.

PART III

GOD'S DESIGN FOR PRAISE & WORSHIP

HOW SHALL
WE PRAISE GOD?
by Dr. Graham Truscott

"Quicken thou me according to thy word...and quicken thou me in thy way" (Psalm 119:25,37).

The answer to the question, "How should we praise God?" is simply, "according to Thy Word ...in Thy Way." We are to praise and worship God and rejoice before Him, in the way He teaches us in His Word.

When the Presence and power of God come among His people, there will always be manifestations of that power and Presence. There will always be spontaneous worship and adoration of the Lord, as there was when the Ark of God came to the Tabernacle of David. And as the Ark of God returns to the Tabernacle of David which God is restoring, there are the same manifestations and the same praise and worship of God today. Some may call this praise and worship fanatical. Others may mock. (One actually did mock at the first Tabernacle of

David — and deeply regretted having done so for the rest of her life). Yet others may even go so far as to call this heresy. The apostle Paul testified: *"But this I confess unto thee, that after the way which they call heresy, so worship I the God of my fathers, believing all things which are written in the law and in the prophets"* (Acts 24:14).

Do all of us today believe *all* things written in the law and the prophets concerning worship? More than this — are we *doing them?*

Others may criticize believing and practising Biblical methods of praise and worship as emotionalism. That Biblical commandments and teachings should be criticized at all is serious enough. But he who can experience the power and Presence of God's amazing love and not have at times his emotions deeply stirred, must be, to say the least, of a very hard heart.

Billy Graham says of emotionalism: "Some people accuse us of too much emotionalism. I say we have too little. This is why we are losing church people to other interests. We need not only to capture their minds, we've got to touch their hearts. We've got to make people feel their faith." [1]

Time Magazine reported (September 27, 1968), under the headline, "That New Black Magic": "As organized religion loses its appeal through its stuffiness and sterility, people seeking faith increasingly turn to mystical religions..."

In 10 years of travelling for Christ through many lands, I have never yet seen a church which worshipped God in Spirit and in truth, practising the Biblical methods of praise and worship, with a decreasing membership.

"How should we praise God?" Here is a list of fourteen Biblical ways by which we are exhorted to praise and worship God. Each one is a God-given expression of worship and adoration to the Lord.

1. PRAISE GOD WITH PRAISE
    WHICH CAN BE HEARD.

    "O bless our God, ye people and make the voice of his praise to be heard" (Psalm 66:8). And how was the voice of His praise to be made audible? The answer is in verse 17: "I cried aloud to Him; He was extolled and high praise was under my tongue" (AMP).

    God commands us in His Word: *"Make a joyful noise unto the Lord...make a LOUD NOISE and rejoice and sing praise"* (Psalm 98:4).

    David said that even when he was praying he "made a *noise*" (see Psalm 55:2). How much more should our praise and worship be heard?

    Thus we see it is not just a matter of worshipping God quietly in our hearts. The Bible commands that our voices be heard praising and worshipping the Lord.

2. PRAISE GOD WITH SHOUTING.

    The Bible commands us to: *"Shout to God with the voice of triumph and songs of joy!"* (Psalm 47:1, AMP). Again the Bible commands: *"Let them shout for joy and be glad, that favour my righteous cause: yea, let them say continually, Let the Lord be magnified..."* (Psalm 35:27).

    Yet again it is written in the psalms of David: *"Let thy priests be clothed with righteousness; and let thy saints shout for joy"* (Psalm 132:9).

    Here again we see emphasized the transition from the legal and ceremonial to the spiritual. David is not so much concerned with the outward form of the priestly garments, but he is vitally concerned that the priests experience the righteousness of God in their lives. Also, he encourages the people to "shout for joy" — vastly different from the silent formality in the Tabernacle of Moses.

    It may not fit in with the mournful silence and decorum

some feel should be seen in the house of God. However, the Bible teaches *"ALL Israel brought up the ark of the covenant of the Lord with shouting..."* (I Chronicles 15:28). And God is restoring the Tabernacle of David with exactly the same expression of praise and worship — shouting.

3. PRAISE GOD WITH SINGING.

"Sing praises to God, sing praises: sing praises unto our King, sing praises" (Psalm 47:6).

The book of Psalms was actually the "Hebrew Hymnal," the *Book of Praises,* hymns, or songs, designed to be set to music and used in the worship of God. A large number of these psalms, or hymns, are "songs of Zion" — songs given by the Spirit of God and recorded at the Tabernacle of David. But during the captivity, the people were not able to sing the joyful songs of Zion (see Psalm 137). And so it is today. Those who are bound, who have not yet fully appreciated *"the glorious liberty of the children of God"* (Romans 8:21) are unable to worship God with spontaneous songs of praise and worship.

New Testament Christians are commanded: *"be filled with the Spirit; speaking to yourselves in psalms and hymns and spiritual songs, singing and making melody in your heart to the Lord; giving thanks always for all things unto God and the Father in the name of our Lord Jesus Christ"* (Ephesians 5:18-20).

No doubt, in the early church, the Old Testament Psalms were used. Several passages of the letter of Paul were used as hymns. Yet many songs were given spontaneously by the Spirit. As Arthur Way says in the preface to his popular translation, *The Letters of Saint Paul:* "Paul tells the Ephesian Christians to 'speak to one another in psalms, in hymns, in chants inspired by the Spirit.' Passages from the Psalms were sung by them no doubt. It is by no means certain that the 'Psalms' referred to are the Psalms of David and it can hardly be so in First Corinthians 14:26. The context shows that the composition of the psalms (or hymns) was one *manifestation of the Gifts of the Spirit.*"

Paul also says: *"I will sing with my spirit — by the Holy Spirit that is within me; but I will sing (intelligently) with my mind and understanding also"* (I Corinthians 14:15 AMP).

What tongue can describe with natural words that which is altogether supernatural? Here words fail us altogether. Who can ever forget being in a congregation with Spirit-filled sons and daughters of God, experiencing the singing lifted up by the Holy Spirit, where the words, melodies and harmonies are all given by the Spirit. Most testify that in such times of worship they know the Presence of God in a very real and special way.

John Sherrill, well-known journalist and a conventional Episcopalian, began, as a journalist, an objective investigation into the recurrence of "speaking with tongues" and other miraculous manifestations of the Holy Spirit in his own and other historic denominations. (John and Elizabeth Sherrill were associated with David Wilkerson in the writing of the widely-read book, *The Cross and The Switch blade.*) He recalls the first time he heard singing in the Spirit: "As the music continued, several people at the tables began to sing 'in the Spirit.' Soon the whole room was singing a complicated harmony-without-score, created spontaneously. It was eerie but extraordinarily beautiful. The song leader was no longer trying to direct the music, but let the melodies create themselves: without prompting one quarter of the room would suddenly start to sing very loudly while others subsided. Harmonies and counter-harmonies wove in and out of each other." [2]

We would in no wise belittle the inspired hymns of Wesley, Luther, Crosby, Alexander and a host of others God has used to write words expressing our praise and worship to Him. But let us also remember that the Lord has provided *two* Spirit-inspired methods by which we may sing unto Him — with our understanding and with our spirits. Let us then *"Praise ye the Lord: for it is good to sing praises unto our God..."* (Psalm 147:1).

4. PRAISE GOD WITH THANKSGIVING.

"I will praise the name of God with a song and will magnify him with thanksgiving" (Psalm 69:30). Thanksgiving is much more than saying grace at the meal table. The Bible says we are to magnify God with thanksgiving. Concerning thanksgiving, we may also note that God may be magnified with thanksgiving in unknown tongues, as the Holy Spirit gives utterance. The Bible teaches *"if you bless and render thanks with [your] spirit [thoroughly aroused by the Holy Spirit]..."* that is, by speaking in unknown tongues (verse 14) — you *"To be sure. . . give thanks well..."* (I Corinthians 14:16,17 AMP). [3]

5. PRAISE GOD WITH A JOYFUL NOISE.

"Make a joyful noise unto God, all ye lands; sing forth the honour of his name: make his praise glorious" (Psalm 66:1,2).

Billy Graham's *Decision* Magazine recently published the following incident from the life of the famous composer, Franz Haydn: "A friend once asked the great composer Haydn why his church music was always so full of gladness. He answered, 'I cannot make it otherwise; I write according to the thoughts I feel; when I think upon my God, my heart is so full of joy, that the notes dance and leap from my pen; and since God has given me a cheerful heart, it will be pardoned me that I serve Him with a cheerful spirit.' "

Let us heed God's invitation: *"O come, let us sing unto the Lord: let us make a joyful noise to the rock of our salvation"* (Psalm 95:1).

How did David and his people bring the Ark of God to Zion? "With joy" (see I Chronicles 15:25), because the very Presence of God dwelt between the cherubim of the ark. Thus God was with them in the power of His Presence and as the Bible says, *"Thou wilt show me the path of life: in thy presence is fulness of joy..."* (Psalm 16:11).

6. PRAISE GOD WITH CRYING OUT.

"Cry out and shout, thou inhabitant of Zion: for great is the Holy One of Israel in the midst of thee" (Isaiah 12:6). It happened in Zion of old, and it happens in spiritual Zion today. When the majesty and greatness of the Presence of God is in the midst of His people, His people cry out their praises and worship to Him.

The famous evangelist, Charles Finney, testified that he "bellowed out," and "cried out" when he received his baptism in the Holy Spirit while alone in his law office on October 10, 1821. He says:

"I then received a mighty baptism of the Holy Ghost. Without any expectation of it, without ever having the thought in my mind that there was such a thing for me, without any recollection that I had ever heard the thing mentioned by any person in the world, the Holy Spirit descended upon me in a manner that seemed to go through me, body and soul. I could feel the impression like a wave of electricity, going through me. Indeed, it seemed to come in waves of liquid love. It seemed like the very breath of God. I can recollect distinctly that it seemed to fan me like immense wings. No words can express the wonderful love that was shed abroad in my heart. I wept aloud with joy and love: and I do not know but I should say, I literally bellowed out the unutterable gushings of my heart. These waves came over me and over me, one after the other, until I cried out, 'I shall die if these waves continue to pass over me.' I said, 'Lord, I cannot bear any more.' Yet I had no fear of death...

"Thus I continued till late at night, when I received some sound repose. When I awoke in the morning the sun had risen and was pouring a clear light into my room. Words cannot express the impression that this sunlight made upon me. Instantly the baptism that I had received the night before returned upon me in the same manner. I arose upon my knees in the bed and wept aloud with joy and remained for some time too much overwhelmed with the baptism of the Spirit to do anything but pour out my soul to God. It seemed as if this morning's baptism was accompanied with a gentle reproof and the Spirit seemed to say to me, 'Will you doubt? Will you doubt?' I cried, 'No! I will not doubt; I cannot doubt.' "

Would to God all who preach the Word today receive such a mighty baptism with the Holy Ghost and fire and be as unashamed to cry out to God as Finney was!

7. PRAISE GOD WITH SPEAKING IN TONGUES.

When the one hundred and twenty were filled with the Spirit on the Day of Pentecost, they were heard praising the Lord in other tongues, telling forth *"the wonderful works of God"* (Acts 2:11). Peter's companions at Caesarea were convinced that Cornelius and his company had received the gift of the Holy Spirit. *"For they heard them speak with tongues and magnify God..."* (Acts 10:46). And as we have already noticed, the Bible teaches the one who worships God in an unknown tongue speaks *"unto God"* and *"givest thanks well"* (I Corinthians 14:2,17).

Jesus said speaking in new tongues was a sign all believers may enjoy (see Mark 16:17). How often those who love the Lord with all their hearts, have been at a loss for words to express their love, praise and adoration to Him. Then the Holy Spirit takes over and the spirit of the believer who has received the baptism with the Holy Ghost praises God. In this way the believer *"who speaks in a [strange] tongue edifies and improves himself..."* (I Corinthians 14:4 AMP). For praise is born in the heart and expressed with the tongue. *"Praise ye the Lord. I will praise the Lord with my whole heart..."* (Psalm 111:1). *"My tongue shall speak...thy praise..."* (Psalm 35:28).

8. PRAISE GOD WITH LAUGHTER.

"When the Lord turned again the captivity of Zion, we were like them that dream. Then was our mouth filled with laughter and our tongue with singing: then said they among the heathen, The Lord hath done great things for them. The Lord hath done great things for us; whereof we are glad" (Psalm 126:1-3).

Laughter in church? Why, say some, the very thought seems sacrilegious. And yet some Christians will laugh at ridiculous, trivial amusements and think nothing of it. The greatest joy in all the world is the joy which Jesus gives — the joy of the Lord. And they laugh, whose heart He makes merry.

One of the greatest outpourings of the Holy Spirit ever to take place in India occurred more than eighty years ago at Kedgaon, 30 miles from Poona. As the Holy Spirit fell at Ramabai Mukti Mission, literal fire was seen. [4] Hundreds were baptized with the Holy Ghost and fire according to the promise of the Lord and hundreds more were saved. Scriptural manifestations of the power of God were witnessed, including shaking, dancing before the Lord, speaking with tongues, laughter, praise and worship and many more. As always, when one section of God's church receives an outpouring of the Spirit, there were criticisms at the manifestations of the power of God. Writing in defence of these, Ramabai refers to praising God with laughter:

"On the day of Pentecost the manifestations were so great that the people mocked, saying, 'These men are full of new wine.' We are told in these days to suppress all manifestations of the Spirit as they are not proper...A young woman in church was on her knees between the pews, when with closed eyes, her mouth was filled with laughter and praise, because of the joy the Lord had poured out upon her. An elder sitting along the same pew saw this and arose demanding that it be stopped, as this was not proper behaviour in the house of God. If these manifestations of the Holy Spirit had been stopped on the day of Pentecost, the crowds of people would not have come together to inquire what had happened and 3,000 people would not have been converted that day. [5]

Make no mistake about it. The restoration of the Tabernacle of David is a restoration of joy. How many of us *need* such a restoration. We should pray with David: *"Restore unto me the joy of thy salvation; and uphold me with thy free spirit"* (Psalm 51:12).

Again David said: *"Because thy lovingkindness is better than life, my lips shall praise thee...my mouth shall praise thee with joyful lips"* (Psalm 63:3,5). Is this your experience too?

9. PRAISE GOD WITH MUSICAL INSTRUMENTS.

As the Ark of the Covenant returned to the people of God, they praised God with almost every musical instrument available. So many Scriptures show we are commanded to praise God with musical instruments (for example, read Psalm 150). And the Bible teaches the musical instruments are to be played "with a loud noise": *"Rejoice in the Lord, O ye righteous: for praise is comely for the upright. Praise the Lord with harp: sing unto him with the psaltery and an instrument of ten strings. Sing unto him a new song; play skillfully with a loud noise"* (Psalm 33:1-3).

10. PRAISE GOD BY BOWING
AND KNEELING BEFORE HIM.

"O come, let us worship and bow down: let us kneel before the Lord our maker" (Psalm 95:6).

This theme is seen also throughout the New Testament. For it is written, *"at the name of Jesus every knee should bow..."* (Philippians 2:10). Paul testified, *"I bow my knees unto the Father of our Lord Jesus Christ"* (Ephesians 3:14). We are commanded to strengthen *"the feeble knees"* (Hebrews 12:12). The Bible teaches kneeling is not just for praying, but also for praising and giving God thanks (e.g. see Daniel 6:10).

11. PRAISE GOD BY FALLING
PROSTRATE BEFORE HIM.

"And Ezra blessed the Lord, the great God. And all the people answered, Amen, Amen, with lifting up their hands: and they bowed their heads and worshipped the Lord with their faces to the ground" (Nehemiah 8:6).

This is not an uncommon sight today where the power of God's Presence is manifested. Indeed, it has been an act of worship whenever God has moved by His Spirit in a mighty way. For example, John Wesley records in his Journal:

"We were present at our love-feast in Fetter Lane with about sixty of our brethren. About three in the morning as we were continuing instant in prayer, the power of God came mightily upon us, inasmuch that many *cried out* for exceeding joy and many *fell to the ground.* As soon as we were recovered a little from that awe and amazement at the presence of His Majesty, we broke out with one voice 'We praise Thee, O God, we acknowledge Thee to be the Lord.' " [6]

Would these early Methodists with their emotional response to the moving of the Holy Spirit in their midst at three o'clock in the morning, be welcomed to some of our dry, formal one-hour services today?

12. PRAISE GOD WITH CLAPPING OF HANDS.

"O clap your hands, all ye people; shout unto God with the voice of triumph" (Psalm 47:1). We clap our hands in appreciation of many things. A good item, a welcome, a good performance in a sporting event. Why then be embarrassed by all clapping hands together unto the Lord as an expression of our appreciation of Him? The Bible commands us to clap our hands unto the Lord.

13. PRAISE GOD WITH THE LIFTING UP OF HANDS.

"Thus will I bless thee while I live: I will lift up my hands in thy name" (Psalm 63:4).

As we have already seen, when Ezra praised God, *"all the people answered, Amen, Amen, with lifting up their hands..."* (Nehemiah 8:6).

There was a lifting up of hands towards the Tabernacle of David. *"I lift up my hands toward the oracle of thy Sanctuary"* (Psalm 28:2). [7]

In the New Testament we read that it is the will of God to "lift up holy hands, without wrath and doubting" (see I Timothy 2:8).

Again, it is written: *"Wherefore lift up the hands which hang down..."* (Hebrews 12:12). The *Amplified Bible* renders this verse: *"So then, brace up and reinvigorate and set right your slackened and weakened and drooping hands..."*

The Lord Jesus lifted up His hands upon the Cross of Calvary for us. Shall we not obey God's Word and lift up our hands in worship to Him? God commands us: *"Lift up your hands in the sanctuary and bless the Lord"* (Psalm 134:2).

14. PRAISE GOD WITH THE DANCE.

"Praise him with the...dance..." (Psalm 150:4). Contrary to what some think, there are many references, in both Old and New Testaments, to rejoicing, praise and worship being expressed in dancing. Dr. Robert Young's *Analytical Concordance to the Holy Bible* lists twenty-seven such references. While it is, as one writer has termed it, "the most extreme form of worship," dancing before the Lord is nevertheless a very blessed and Scriptural method of demonstrating our adoration of God. Only a few examples are given here.

Moses sang a song of praise for the deliverance of the people from Egypt through the Red Sea (in which incidentally, is probably the first reference to the Tabernacle of David on Zion — Exodus 15:17). After this, his sister Miriam, together with all the women, praised God with dancing: *"And Miriam the prophetess, the sister of Aaron, took a timbrel in her hand; and all the women went out after her with timbrels and with dances. And Miriam answered them, Sing ye to the Lord, for he hath triumphed gloriously; the horse and his rider hath he thrown into the sea"* (Exodus 15:20,21).

Gideon and his 300 men knew the value of praise. For when they cried out and shouted, breaking their pitchers and blowing their trumpets, the enemy was dismayed. Gideon and his men pursued the Midianites to Abel-meholah and it was there the enemy was defeated. *Abel-meholah* means *"the meadow of the dance."*

One of King Solomon's twelve officers appointed over his food was to supply provisions for one month of the year from Abel-meholah, the meadow of the dance (see I Kings 4:7,12). And today, dancing before the Lord is part of the table spread for us by the greater than Solomon, the Lord Jesus Christ.

Elisha the prophet, who received the double portion of the spirit of Elijah, was born at Abel-Meholah, the meadow of the dance (see I Kings 19:16). God grant that today many more

Elishas be born in the revival times of praise and worship, including dancing before the Lord.

When the Tabernacle of Moses was at Shiloh, the daughters of Shiloh came *"out to dance in dances"* at certain feast days unto the Lord. *"The children of Benjamin...took them wives, according to their number, of them that danced..."* (Judges 21:19-23). At certain times of the year, during the feasts unto the Lord, dancing was an integral part of rejoicing before Him in praise and worship. And today, *"the people who know the joyful sound [who understand and appreciate the spiritual blessings symbolized by the feasts]..."* (Psalm 89:15 AMP) also know the blessing of dancing before the Lord in expression of their love and praise to Him.

Dancing before the Lord was a customary part of victory processions in the Old Testament. For example, when David was victorious over the Philistines: *"And it came to pass as they came, when David was returned from the slaughter of the Philistine, that the women came out of all cities of Israel, singing and dancing, to meet king Saul with tabrets, with joy and with instruments of musick"* (I Samuel 18:6; see also I Samuel 21:11; 29:5).

Turning to the New Testament, we read that the father commanded music and dancing and making merry at the return of his prodigal son (see Luke 15:22-25). (Let us be careful not to react as the prodigal elder brother did).

But so many of us today could be described in the words of our Lord: *"We have piped unto you and ye have not danced..."* (Matthew 11:17).

Dr. Edwin Orr has said in his book, *Full Surrender:* "Now I share with Dr. Ironside, the view, that if a Christian is happy and feels like dancing, there is no reason why he should not go to his room or another suitable place and dance before the Lord!" [8]

The Preacher declares: *"There is ... a time to mourn and a time to dance"* (Ecclesiastes 3:1,4). Do you dance before the Lord with joy?

a) *The Meaning of Dancing*

The various Hebrew and Greek words from which our English word "dance" comes, have various shades of meaning which explain to us what this dancing before the Lord is. They are *to keep festival, to turn, twist; to move around; to lift up the feet; to skip and leap.*

When the lame man was healed at the gate of the temple in Acts chapter 3, he entered into the temple walking and leaping and praising God (see Acts 3:8). The crippled man at Lystra also leaped when he was healed (see Acts 14:10). Look up all the references to leaping in the Bible. You will find this an interesting and rewarding study.

The great English translator of the Bible, William Tyndale (who was later arrested and burned at the stake for his reformer's zeal), defined the Gospel thus: "EUAGELIO (that we call Gospel) is a Greek word and signifies good, merry, glad and joyful tidings, that maketh a man's heart glad and maketh him sing, dance and leap for joy." [9]

Above all, hear the words of Jesus: *"Rejoice ye in that day and leap for joy: for, behold, your reward is great in heaven: for in the like manner did their fathers unto the prophets"* (Luke 6:23).

There it is. The commandment of our Master. The Lord Jesus also said we were to love God with all our strength. And it takes all our strength to leap and dance before Him in worship, adoration and praise (see Mark 12:30).

b) *The Restoration of Praising God*
   with the Dance.

When the people of God were in captivity, the prophet Jeremiah lamented. *"The joy of our heart is ceased; our dance is turned into mourning"* (Lamentations 5:15).

But the Lord revealed by His Spirit that there was coming a

day of restoration. Concerning this day of restoration, God said: *"in the latter days ye shall consider it" (Amplified* — understand this) (Jeremiah 30:24).

Then the Lord speaks of the wonderful rebuilding of which we have spoken so much: *"At the same time,* (the latter days — chapter 30:24) *saith the Lord...'Again I will build thee and thou shalt be built, O virgin of Israel: thou shalt again be adorned with thy tabrets and shalt go forth in the dances of them that make merry...Then shall the virgin rejoice in the dance, both young men and old together: for I will turn their mourning into joy and will comfort them and make them rejoice from their sorrow"* (Jeremiah 31:1,4,13).

Dancing before the Lord is a direct result of this last day restoration revival — an expression of rejoicing in the Lord, praising God for all His goodness. This is particularly true of the restoration of the Tabernacle of David in these last days.

When the power of the Presence of God above the Ark of the Covenant came to Zion, David danced before the Lord: *"David danced before the Lord with all his might..."* (II Samuel 6:14).

In spite of all the blessings David had experienced from God, he still mourned and lamented after the fulness of the power of God's Presence. When he brought up the Ark of God to Zion, he testified that God turned his mourning into dancing: *"Thou hast turned for me my mourning into dancing: thou hast put off my sackcloth and girded me with gladness: To the end that my tongue* [10] may sing praise to thee and not be silent. O Lord my God, I will give thanks unto thee for ever"* (Psalm 30:11,12).

And those who would take part in the restoration of the Tabernacle of David, the children of Zion, are commanded to praise God with dancing: *"let the children of Zion be joyful in their King. Let them praise His name in the dance..."* (Psalm 149:2,3).

This article is used by permission of Dr. Graham Truscott from his book *The Power of His Presence* (Restoration Temple: San Diego, CA).

Footnotes:

1. *The Quotable Billy Graham* (Murray Publishing Company).
2. *They Speak With Other Tongues*, by John L. Sherrill, (Hodder and Stoughton).
3. However, single or solitary outbursts in tongues must be interpreted, in the church, that the whole church may be edified.
4. For a fuller description of the revival, at Kedgaon, see chapter 14, "It Happened in India" of the author's book, *You Shall Receive Power.*
5. *The Baptism of the Holy Ghost and Fire* (printed at the "Mukti Mission" Press) 1906, by Pandita Ramabai.
6. *John Wesley's Journal*, Vol. I. Monday, January 1, 1739 (emphasis ours).
7. Marginal rendering.
8. From *Full Surrender* by J. Edwin Orr (Marshall, Morgan & Scott). It was in Dr. Orr's meetings in St. Paul's Presbyterian Church, Christchurch, New Zealand, in 1956, that the author first clearly came to understand that the fulness with the Spirit is a second operation of the Spirit, as distinct from conversion. It was a joy and blessing to have him stay in our home in India ten years later.

    There are many other "suitable places" where we may dance before the Lord; for example, the house of God.
9. As quoted in *Decision*, May 1968.
10. Marginal rendering.

WEAPONS
OF WORSHIP
by Dr. David K. Blomgren

A s God's people gather to worship Him they have the power and authority, which comes from God's glory being released, to be a destroying, consuming force against God's enemies. Let us look at some Biblical proof of this.

WORSHIP WARFARE

The power of worship is illustrated in the events of Joshua 6, when the children of Israel, under Joshua's leadership, were led to march around the city of Jericho until the time came to shout in triumph before the Lord. The priests led in worship, playing the trumpets as Joshua directed and a great battle was won.

In that battle the people of Israel had become, by their shouts and the sound of the trumpet, a "rereward" (vv. 9,13), a gathered people who had the power to destroy the enemy. All they had to do was shout together. As they did this, the walls came down and the enemy was defeated.

The word "rereward" has the meaning in the Hebrew "to gather in order to destroy or consume." This is the same Hebrew word for the name of Asaph, who was the man appointed by David in I Chronicles 16:37 *"To minister before the ark continually..."* He was responsible for those who were appointed to minister before the ark in the Tabernacle of David.

In these last days, as God restores the Tabernacle of David, He is again appointing us as Asaphs, to gather together and worship Him in His presence, before His glory. Isaiah 58:8b promises that *"the glory of the Lord shall be thy rereward"* (Hebrew "asaph"). As we minister in Tabernacle of David worship, God's glory is revealed as our rereward. We become a gathered company whose worship becomes warfare to destroy the enemy.

The concept of God's glory as a rereward thus includes the principle of warfare. This is also illustrated in Numbers 4:23, where the Lord is speaking to Moses about those who are appointed to be priests. He described them as being all those who *"enter in to perform the service..."* The words "perform the service" are from Hebrew words which mean, literally, "fight the warfare." "Perform" is the translation of the Hebrew word "tsaba," from which we get "sabaoth" and "hosts" (as in "Lord of Hosts," a name with strong military overtones; see Psalm 24:8,10). The priests entered into the holy place to fight a warfare.

We see the same words used in the original of Numbers 8:24, which is translated *"to wait upon the service..."* Clearly, the priests were appointed to fight a spiritual warfare against God's enemies.

The same principle is carried on throughout Scripture. In the New Testament as well we find that God's people are not just to minister before the Lord in liturgical and religious duties, but they are to engage in warfare as they carry out their service to the Lord. This principle is exemplified best in the Tabernacle of David, where God calls and appoints "Asaphs" to minister continually before Him.

Each aspect of worship in the Tabernacle of David produces a power which God uses to crush His enemies. Therefore, each part of our worship becomes a weapon of warfare.

THE SONG OF PRAISE

In our singing, when we sing new songs of praise as they did in the Tabernacle of David, we are exercising authority as king-priests over the enemy. In Psalm 27:5-6 David declares that in his times of trouble, God gives him victory through sacrifices of joy — singing praises unto God. He clearly expects that as he sings songs of praise unto the Lord, his head shall *"be lifted up above mine enemies..."*

(Notice in verse 5 of Psalm 27 that David has learned the need for refuge in the house of the Lord in times of trouble. When we face times of trouble, we need to learn that God's covering and hiding place is in the house of the Lord, the tabernacle that David sought for protection.)

When we see in these verses the words "sacrifices of joy," we need to keep in mind that we are dealing in the original language with only one Hebrew word. "Terou'a" is a Hebrew word which soldiers used as a war cry or battle cry when they were going to battle. In this verse, David is sounding the battle cry, leading his people into warfare as their captain, *"a leader and commander to the people"* (Isaiah 55:4b). Such a cry would be a shout of confidence that the battle was going to be won. It was designed to cause the enemy to fear their strength.

I believe that God gave David a revelation here — that God's people should express the same confidence of victory that warriors express when going into battle. David understood that as God's people come to sing new songs of praise, lifting their voices to Him, that praise rises to the Lord to exalt Him as well as going against the enemy. Satan hears it as a triumphant battle cry against him and that causes him to fear.

Christ has "spoiled principalities and powers" and has made a show of them openly to demonstrate that He has already triumphed over them (see Colossians 2:15). The word "spoiled" in this verse is from the Greek word "apekduomai," which comes from the word "ekduo." Ekduo means to strip or unclothe something. Apekduomai carried this thought further, in that it was a hunting term which meant to skin and stuff a kill.

God has spoiled Satan — He has unclothed him and left him naked. He has taken the hide right off of him. He has made a show of him openly and has triumphed over him. The enemy is defeated!

As we sing new songs of praise to God, we are sounding the battle cry of the host of God. Satan hears that sound and knows he is entering a battle which he is going to lose. He has already faced the Captain of the host of God and has been defeated!

THE VICTORY SHOUT

We have already seen that God brought a great victory to the children of Israel when they went against the city of Jericho. Notice in Joshua 6:16,20-21 that Joshua instructed the people to shout at his command and as they shouted, God gave them the city. The word translated "shout" in this verse is, again, the Hebrew word "terou'a." As they shouted they sounded a battle cry against the enemy and nothing was able to stand before them.

The men of Judah kept in mind the power they had in shouting before the Lord in battle, even when the situation appeared hopeless. *"And when Judah looked back, behold, the battle was before and behind: and they cried unto the Lord and the priests sounded with trumpets. Then the men of Judah gave a shout: and AS THE MEN OF JUDAH SHOUTED, it came to pass, that God smote Jeroboam and all Israel before Abijah and Judah. And the children of Israel fled before Judah: and God delivered them into their hand"* (II Chronicles 13:14-16). Judah had been caught in a trap with no way of escape, but God turned their certain defeat into a victory as they shouted unto Him.

Psalm 149:6-9 describes the two offensive weapons of the believer's armour: the two-edged sword and the high praises of God. Through the exercise of these two weapons, we are told, the saints will execute vengeance against the enemy and punishments upon the people; kings will be bound in chains and nobles in iron fetters. I believe that these are to be the results of our spiritual battles against spiritual enemies. We wrestle against principalities and powers and spiritual wickedness in high places (Ephesians 6:12). The power of the enemy has been destroyed and they have been delivered into our hands.

Whenever God's people come together to praise Him with singing, shouting and audible praise and worship, they are sounding the battle cry which destroys the power of the enemy. I believe there is power in our worship which we do not yet fully understand and have failed to fully use.

It is as we realize that we have a heavy weight of responsibility to come before the Lord as a pure priesthood, in obedience, praising and worshipping Him, that we will be battling the enemy with power and effectiveness.

LIFTING HANDS

There are other elements of worship and praise which are also to be used as weapons of warfare. One of these is the lifting of holy hands in worship (see Psalm 134:2).

We see an example of the lifting of hands in worship during a battle in Exodus 17:9-11. In this passage, Moses calls the people of God to warfare against the Amalekites. We find in verse 11 that so long as Moses' hands were lifted before the Lord, Israel prevailed over her enemies. When he became weary, however and his arm started to drop, the enemy began to win.

When we lift our hands unto the Lord, we are not just performing an optional form of worship that we can take or leave, depending on how we feel. As we lift our hands in worship we are utilizing a very powerful weapon against the enemy, which causes God's people to prevail. It is only when we are not reaching out to God, as when Moses' hands dropped, that the enemy prevails.

Sometimes our hands do become heavy, however and we don't feel like reaching out to God in worship. When that happens, we have to get our hands back up, even if we have to have an Aaron and a Hur help us. As we do so, the enemy will be driven back and defeated.

However, if we fail to strengthen ourselves for battle and become "weary in well-doing" the enemy will overtake us and the result will be a defeat when there could have been victory.

We should be a people of life and victory. Let us reach our hands out to God and allow Him to prevail over the enemy.

CLAPPING HANDS

In Old Testament times clapping was used as a means of mocking the enemy when the battle was soon to begin. We see this illustrated in Lamentations 2:15, which speaks of God's enemies clapping their hands in derision against the inhabitants of Jerusalem.

Clapping was also used as an expression of the victory God has given over the enemy (see Psalm 47:1). It is therefore used both as a means of honouring God and as a hissing and mocking against the enemy, declaring that he is a defeated foe.

MUSICAL INSTRUMENTS

Most of us are familiar with how David's playing of his

harp before King Saul eased the power of the evil spirit to plague Saul. Saul had been under demonic attack because of his sin and rebellion and the playing of David's instrument was the only thing which gave him deliverance from that attack (see I Samuel 16:23).

This illustrates the principle that the playing of an instrument, under God's anointing, is a powerful weapon of warfare against the enemy. This is confirmed in Psalm 33:3b, where the righteous are commanded to *"play skillfully with a loud noise."* The words "loud noise" are from the Hebrew word "terou'a," the same word which, as we saw earlier, was used for the battle cry against an enemy.

Therefore, worshipping the Lord on our instruments is equally as important as singing and other forms of worship. As the instrument is played before the Lord, under His anointing, it sounds a battle cry against the enemy from which the enemy flees.

STANDING AND BOWING

It is interesting to note that the only position not mentioned in the Psalms with reference to worship is sitting. Psalm 134:1 speaks of God's servants standing by night in the house of the Lord; in II Chronicles 20:19 we read that when the Levites in the Tabernacle of David praised the Lord, they stood to do so.

Throughout Scripture, this posture is seen as one showing a readiness to stand with the Lord in warfare.

Bowing is another form of worship noted in Scripture, one which recognizes God's sovereignty and holiness. The Hebrew word translated "worship," "shachah," literally means "to bow down or to fall down." Psalm 72:9 describes people in the wilderness bowing before the Lord. These are the enemies of God, who shall be forced to "lick the dust." Even God's enemies are not exempt from the requirement to bow before Him and eventually every knee shall do so (see Philippians 2:10).

God's people are to be a worshipping people, who willingly acknowledge by standing and by bowing His sovereignty over their lives and their willingness to make Him their Lord and their Commander in battle. We are not to dwell in the wilderness with the enemies of God. Rather, we are to stand with the Lord in defeating His enemies, as an act of spiritual warfare.

DANCING

In Exodus 15:20, we see that Miriam led the nation in the dance as a celebration of the victory God had accomplished over His enemies. She was thereby acknowledging His hand in victory, as He threw the horses and riders of Egypt into the sea.

Psalm 149:3 and 150:4 command God's people to praise the Lord in the dance. This is because dancing is not just an act of worship, but an act of warfare against God's enemies, speaking of God's crushing of the enemy under His feet (see Psalm 110:1).

WOUNDING THE ENEMY'S HEAD

Habakkuk 3:13b speaks of God wounding *"the head out of the house of the wicked, by discovering* (literally "making naked") *the foundation unto the neck..."* So powerful is the worship of God's people that their words are as mighty arrows shot forth into the air which shine with the brilliance of God's glory (see v. 11). They strike the enemy at the foundation of his head, separating the head from the body of the wicked and sending the body into confusion, thereby rendering it powerless.

God is today restoring His glory in Zion, as He restores the pattern of praise and worship of David's Tabernacle. He is calling us to be priests, bearing the heavy responsibility of serving Him in purity; His desire is to release His power to us as a royal priesthood. As we receive the power of God's glory, let us come against the enemy, both individually and collectively, as a mighty, conquering army of God. We will have a great victory, for the battle is the Lord's and the battle has already been won!

THE JEHOSHAPHAT PROCESS
by Steve Griffing

King Jehoshaphat *"appointed singers unto the Lord and that should praise the beauty of holiness, as they went out before the army...And when they began to sing and to praise, the Lord set ambushments against the children of Ammon, Moab and mount Seir, which were come against Judah; and they were smitten.*

"And when Judah came...they looked unto the multitude and, behold, they were dead bodies fallen to the earth and none escaped" (II Chronicles 20:21,22,24).

This striking passage of Scripture recounts one of Judah's most spectacular and unusual military victories. Instead of using normal weapons of warfare, Jehoshaphat employed an army of musicians and singers to spearhead the attack and secure a resounding victory. While it is clear that this victory was the result of Sovereign intervention, it is also clear that there is a relationship between the musical craft and the ministry of deliverance. One is left with the distinct impression that this account must contain principles of worship that could benefit the church.

When we examine the events surrounding Jehoshaphat's victory, we *are* able to extract such principles. The actions of Jehoshaphat and Judah as recorded in II Chronicles 17-20 are examples that give us insight into how to gain victory in the spiritual realm. Let us examine briefly each phase of the "Jehoshaphat process" to make it more profitable to us.

PREPARATION AND TRAINING

"And Asa...died...And Jehoshaphat his son reigned in his stead...And the Lord was with Jehoshaphat, because he walked in the first ways of his father David..." (II Chronicles 16:13; 17:1,3). Here is the beginning of Jehoshaphat's success. God was with him because of his commitment to pattern his life and administration after that of David. Like David, he desired to put the Lord at the center of his life and the life of the nation.

This desire is illustrated in the way Jehoshaphat set out to purify and strengthen worship. Verse 6 of chapter 17 shows that following Davidic principles produced a zeal for purity in worship: *"And his heart was lifted up in the ways of the Lord: moreover he took away the high places and groves out of Judah."* This was a critical step in the process.

Also, a military build-up was initiated at the local level *"in all the fenced* (walled) *cities of Judah"* (II Chronicles 17:1-2). This was important for establishing peace and security in the nation, which would create a good atmosphere for worshipping and serving God. "Judah" means "praise," so the cities of Judah can be seen as local habitations of praise — local churches; therefore the strengthening of Judah's cities was like the strengthening of praising local churches. God is placing spiritual "forces" in our modern day "cities of Judah," so that churches emphasizing Biblical forms of praise and worship have a strong defence against the attack of the enemy.

Jehoshaphat also launched a national teaching campaign in the cities of Judah. II Chronicles 15:3 tells how for a long season Israel had been without a "teaching priest." However, with the restoration of Davidic principles God released that ministry. Jehoshaphat sent priests and Levites who *"went about throughout all the cities of Judah and taught the people"* (II Chronicles 17:9).

It is both interesting and vital to note that the Levites were sent to aid in the teaching. One of their chief responsibilities in the Davidic order was to provide the musical medium (compare I Chronicles 16:4,37-42 with I Chronicles 25). This music ministry was coupled with the teaching ministry: "(The musicians) *cast lots for their duties, small and great, teacher and scholar alike"* (I Chronicles 25:8, AMP). Other passages of Scripture, as well as evidence from Jewish writing, confirm that Scripture was rarely rendered without cantillation (musical recitation). Nehemiah 8:8 says the Levites *"read in the book of the law of God distinctly and gave the sense and caused them to understand the reading."* "'Reading distinctly' is a clear indication of a rhythmic articulation and melodious inflection of the spoken word, which according to the Oriental conception are indispensable for an expressive declamation" (A. Sendrey, *Music in Ancient Israel,* London, 1969, p. 211). Thus music was an integral part of the training process.

RESULTS OF PREPARATION

Notice the initial results of Jehoshaphat's preparations and training: The kingdoms round about feared the Lord and made no war against Judah (II Chronicles 17:10) and the kingdom moved into a period of prosperity (II Chronicles 17:11-12). When we follow David's God-glorifying principles we can expect these things to be accomplished (see Psalm 72 and 68:29). The national teaching campaign had taught Judah to use the high praise of God and the two-edged sword to bind the power of kings (compare Psalm 149:6-9 and Ephesians 6:17). They began to live in victory and peace.

One level of maturity in God is to be able to turn back the work of Satan in our lives, but God's perfect will for us is that we walk in peace, not continually having to struggle to achieve victory. Instead of healing, we experience Divine health. Instead of deliverance, we live in Divine order and holiness. Instead of being set free from depression, we live a joyous Christian life. Instead of praying only during crisis, we live a life of prayer.

II Chronicles 18 describes how Jehoshaphat took it upon himself to contribute to God's plan of peace and prosperity. Somehow Jehoshaphat came to the conclusion that extra "insurance" was needed that the ungodly king Ahab could provide. This error almost cost him his life in one battle and eventually brought about a second confrontation, which we looked at in the beginning of this article.

II Chronicles 19 shows how Jehoshaphat was restored after his brush with death. His commitment to God's principles had been tested in battle, but because he had prepared his heart and the nation to seek God (II Chronicles 19:3) the revival carried on. Nevertheless, Jehoshaphat would still have to reap the consequences of his disobedience (II Chronicles 19:2).

INTERCESSION

Judah's enemies came against Jehoshaphat the second time to fight the unusual battle described in II Chronicles 20. This would be another test to check how much Jehoshaphat and Judah had learned. This kind of testing actually strengthens the work of God in much the same way that steel is strengthened by heat, when it is properly applied (compare Isaiah 48:10). When we withstand the test, not only are *we* convinced that God's work is real and effective, but Satan also is convinced!

Faced with the certainty of total genocide and hideous atrocities unless he and his people experienced a Sovereign, miraculous deliverance, Jehoshaphat again followed David's pattern — he set his face to seek the Lord. Notice his great humility in verse 12 as he publicly recognized his complete dependency on the King of kings for the answer to their desperate situation. God is the only true authority; the king only stands as a vicarious symbol of authority for the people's sake. This attitude had been the cornerstone of David's reign as well. In any crisis we need not know *what* the solution is, but *Who* it is!

The focus throughout Jehoshaphat's intercession is heavenward. Like David in Psalm 24, he realized that it is "the generation of them that seek God's face," those who have ascended the hill of God's presence in worship with clean hands and a pure heart, who shall receive blessing from the Lord (compare Psalm 133). To such as these, He is *"The Lord strong and mighty, the Lord mighty in battle"* (Psalm 24:8).

PROPHECY

God begins to intervene in the situation by causing the Spirit of prophecy to flow. *"Then upon Jahaziel...a Levite of the sons of Asaph, came the Spirit of the Lord in the midst of the congregation"* (II Chronicles 20:14). Being that Jahaziel was one of the musicians, this turn of events suddenly assigns greater importance to our music ministry than we may have ever expected. Our yielding of our abilities in music can actually be used to initiate the sound of God's voice in the midst of crisis.

I Chronicles 25:1-3 tells us that *"David and the captains of the host separated to the service the sons of Asaph,...which prophesied according to the order of the king...(They)prophesied with a harp, to give thanks and to praise the Lord."* David knew from ministering to Saul that God's people can sing a "song of *deliverance"* to those in crisis. He wrote, *"thou shalt preserve me from trouble; thou shalt compass me about with songs of deliverance"* (Psalm 32:7).

"And (Jahaziel) *said,...the battle is not yours, but God's...Ye shall not need to fight in this battle: set yourselves, stand ye still and see the salvation of the Lord with you..."* (II Chronicles 20:15-17). Because Jehoshaphat and Judah were prepared in their hearts, they believed God's prophet. Immediately, they fell before the Lord and worshipped Him (v. 18). Music had opened the door to deliverance and with praise and worship the people went right on through the door. As described at the opening of this article, the musicians led the way into the battle; in fact Jahaziel, the one who had delivered the prophecy, may well have been the first one to test the validity of the prophecy in battle!

THE WAR CRY

When Jehoshaphat became a worshipper, his vision was lifted above the natural level. His eyes were anointed so that he saw the elevated, heavenly overview. He saw from God's point of view possibilities that escape normal human consideration. He saw how God could intervene for Judah if they just kept their hearts right and trusted in Him.

Psalm 47:1b says we are to *"shout unto God with the voice of triumph."* Perhaps God directed Jehoshaphat to do just that. Perhaps Jehoshaphat comprehended that God literally inhabits our praise of Him (Psalm 22:3), which means that when we praise Him in the face of crisis, we bring Him onto the battlefield. He may have foreseen that in this way God would set "ambushments" on their behalf. Whatever the case was, Jehoshaphat sent the musicians out first and triumph resulted.

All church music is not strictly worship music. Some is not adoration of God as much as it is directed to scatter the enemy. There is a group of songs that calls the church to arise, prepare for and go to war (for example, "The Army of the Lord" and "God's Got an Army"). In another group are marching and victorious songs (for example, "In the Name of Jesus" and "Through Our God We Shall Do Valiantly"). Our victory is assured by the blood of the Lamb and the word of our testimony (see Revelation 12:11).

THE VICTORY CELEBRATION

After the battle Jehoshaphat and his people *"assembled themselves in the valley of Berachah* ("blessing"); *for there they blessed the Lord..."* (II Chronicles 20:26). They were delirious with joy because the Lord had won the victory for them and they expressed that joy with great Davidic rejoicing and pageantry (vv. 27-28).

Nehemiah 8:10 explains that the joy of the Lord is our strength and many other Scriptures (Psalm 126, for instance) confirm this truth. Joyous praise and rejoicing strengthened the people, reinforcing the faith they had gained by conquering through praise. Their victory celebration contributed to maintaining peace and helped to preserve their dominion. *"So the realm of Jehoshaphat was quiet: for his God gave him rest round about"* (II Chronicles 20:30).

Thus we see a pattern in the "Jehoshaphat process." As worshippers we all engage in the process of spiritual warfare. Jehoshaphat's actions —preparation and training, intercession, the prophetic word, the war cry and the victory celebration — show that worship and specifically the Davidic order of music, plays a part in each phase of spiritual battle. As we move into and declare the victory we have in Christ Jesus, we will be able to rejoice with Jehoshaphat over all our enemies.

RELEASING
CHARISMATIC WORSHIP
by Barry Griffing

"**B**e filled with the Spirit; speaking to yourselves in psalms and hymns and spiritual songs..." (Ephesians 5:18-19). In this definitive passage on corporate worship, the apostle Paul shares with his new Gentile converts in Ephesus a goal and method of Christ-centred liturgy. One of the goals of true corporate worship is to "be filled with the Spirit" — to experience the Spirit-filled Presence of the Lord. The method is to progress from psalms, to hymns, to spiritual songs.

Normal New Testament worship *is* charismatic. A worship service that fails to bring us into God's manifest Presence has "fallen short of the glory." But we should not think that Spirit-filled worship is the monopoly of the New Testament era. True worshippers of the Old Testament recognized the importance of experiencing God's Presence, as well. In Psalm 63:1-2 David asserted that he would seek God continually until he could sense His Presence, spirit, soul and body:

> *O God, You are my God;*
> *Early will I seek You;*
> *MY SOUL thirsts for You;*
> *MY FLESH longs for You;*
> *In a dry and thirsty land*
> *Where there is no water.*
> *So I have looked for You*
> *IN THE SANCTUARY,*
> *To see YOUR POWER*
> *and YOUR GLORY* (NKJV*).

Worship in David's Tabernacle was a dynamic, life-changing, strength-conferring experience. Psalm 84:7 states that true worshippers go FROM STRENGTH TO STRENGTH as they appear before God in Zion. David's exhortation in I Chronicles 16:11 is just as applicable today as it was 3,000 years ago — *"Seek the Lord AND HIS STRENGTH; seek His face evermore."*

SHEDDING OLD GARMENTS

The goal of the worship leader is to bring the congregational worshippers into a corporate awareness of God's manifest Presence. In most cases this will necessitate the putting off of the old garment of traditionalism before putting on the garment of praise. Here are three "old garments" which need to be shed:

1) *Historical Church Traditionalism:* The goal of worship in this setting is *aesthetics* in its order, architecture, music, etc.;
2) *Evangelical Traditionalism:* The goal of worship is to *prepare the audience* for the saving power of God's Word;
3) *Pentecostal Traditionalism:* The goal of worship is to be spontaneously responsive to the prompting of the Holy Spirit.

These three brands of traditionalism each harbor an element

92

of truth. But the pursuit of any one of these as a primary goal of worship will usually exclude the other two. For instance, the Bible certainly commands us to *"worship the Lord in THE BEAUTY OF HOLINESS"* (see Psalm 96:9, I Chronicles 16:29, etc.). However, we can conduct our worship in perfect, beautiful liturgical order and still walk out of the service unconverted, unrefreshed, or unhealed.

Likewise, the conversion of unbelievers should certainly be a hallmark of Christian worship gatherings. But there are risks in making the sermon and altar call the goal of our church meetings. In such services the corporate praise tends to be a rushed, superficial warm-up for the preacher's sermon. The theme of the prepared and congregational music tends to be aimed at the unbeliever rather than at the Lord. If the theme of the music and sermon is exhorted fifty-two weeks a year, then the church continually sacrifices the spiritual nurturing of the ninety-nine for the one lost sheep. By contrast, Paul assures the Corinthians that conversion should be an expected by-product of charismatic worship, *not* dependent upon a sermon and "altar call;" *"Therefore if THE WHOLE CHURCH comes together in one place and...ALL PROPHESY and AN UNBELIEVER or an uninformed person comes in, he is convinced by all...and thus the secrets of his heart are revealed; and so, falling down on his face, he will worship God and report that GOD IS TRULY AMONG YOU...Whenever you come together, EACH OF YOU has a psalm, has a teaching, has a tongue, has a revelation, has an interpretation. Let all things be done FOR EDIFICATION* (of the congregation — not the exhortation of the sinner!)*"* (I Corinthians 14:23-26).

Classic pentecostals see acts of worship as spontaneous responses to the leading of the Holy Spirit. Spontaneity is certainly a Scriptural ingredient woefully missing from most historical and evangelical churches. Jesus stated that the Father seeks worshippers who will worship Him *in spirit* and in truth (see John 4:23,24). Nonetheless, pentecostals depart from "worship in truth" if they throw out *prepared sacrifices of praise and a prepared order of worship*. King David, the quintessential Scriptural praiser, considered preparation to be prerequisite for God's presence. But David had learned the hard way.

PREPARATION

In I Chronicles 13 David failed to *prepare a place* for the Ark of God's Presence, deciding to simply house the ark in his own dwelling *"How shall I bring the ark of God HOME to me?"* I Chronicles 13:12, KJV. Second, he failed to *prepare a people* to bear the Ark of God's Presence *("So they carried the ark of God on a new cart...and Uzza and Ahio drove the cart"* I Chronicles 13:7).

Third, David failed to *prepare an "order of worship"* for bringing up the ark. We see in I Chronicles 13:9 that the "paraders of the lost ark" got off the beaten path to Jerusalem and wandered into Chidon's farm. There was no prepared "parade route," and the results were disastrous: *"And when they came to CHIDON'S THRESHING FLOOR...the oxen stumbled. Then the anger of the Lord was aroused against Uzza and He struck him because he put his hand to the ark; and he died there..."* (I Chronicles 13:9-10).

Fortunately, David didn't let these discouraging developments derail him from his goal of bringing up the ark. In I Chronicles 15 he made adjustments to correct his lack of preparation in I Chronicles 13. First of all, he *prepared a place* for the Presence *("David...PREPARED A PLACE for the ark of God and pitched a tent for it"* I Chronicles 15:1. Second, David *prepared a people* to bear the Presence and minister continually in the prepared place *("Then David said, 'No one may carry the ark of God but the Levites, for the Lord has chosen them TO CARRY THE ARK OF GOD and TO MINISTER BEFORE HIM forever"* I Chronicles 15:2).

ORDER

Third in David's preparations, he *prepared an "order of worship"* that his "paraders of the lost ark" were to follow up to Zion (*"The Lord our God broke out against us, because we did not consult Him about the proper* (due) *order"* I Chronicles 15:13). In fact, I Chronicles 15 goes into considerable detail outlining the order of this glorious parade:

1) David and the elders, captains and high priests, followed by
2) Chenaniah, the songleader, followed by
3) Asaph, Heman and Ethan (singer-conductors), followed by
4) eight Levite singing-lyricists, followed by
5) six Levite singing-harpists, followed by
6) seven priest-trumpeters, followed by
7) two Levite banner-bearers ("door-keepers"), followed by
8) the ark, borne by four Levite-bearers.

(Incidentally, another interesting contrast between I Chronicles 13 and 15 involves the music. In I Chronicles 13:8 the music appears to be spontaneous, unrehearsed congregational music; in I Chronicles 15 it appears to be a combination of *prepared* music (v. 22) and *spontaneous* music (v. 28)!)

What was the result of all this preparation and "due order?" Glorious, Spirit-led spontaneity! King David *"danced before the Lord with all his might..."* (II Samuel 6:14) and *"all Israel brought up the ark with shouting and with the sound of the horn, with trumpets and with cymbals, making music with stringed instruments..."* (I Chronicles 15:28). We see from this that preparation and "due order" don't hinder responsiveness to God's Spirit —they release it.

PREPARATION TODAY

For the contemporary worship leader, preparation is two-fold: inward and outward. God congratulated Jehoshaphat for preparing his heart to seek God (see II Chronicles 19:3). In II Chronicles 5, the Levite musicians who *"came out of the Most*

Holy Place...had sanctified themselves..." (vv. 11,12). We who are called to be worship leaders must sanctify (separate) *ourselves*, physically, mentally and emotionally unto our ministry.

We can inwardly prepare our hearts by coming to the place of worship early to seek God in *pre-service prayer* (compare II Chronicles 29:20). During that time, we crowd everything else out of our minds and begin to sing to God "with the spirit" until our understanding becomes fruitful. As we "stir up" the Holy Spirit within us while waiting on God, direction for the worship service will begin to surface to our conscious minds — song titles, Scriptures, images, etc. During pre-service prayer it's good to keep a notebook with you to jot these things down.

Here are four practical areas of outward preparation that are prerequisites for powerful praise:

1. *Personnel* Make sure you utilize a *worship leading team* and confirm their availability a week in advance. You should also confirm (where applicable) your Overhead Transparency Librarian and your Sound Engineer.

2. *Program* Make a list of songs that your worship leading team is likely to sing. Group them by *key* and *tempo* into medleys. Identify which medleys are best suited for beginning the song service (the "call to worship"). If possible, make photocopies of music, chord charts, etc., for newer songs on the list.

3. *Practice* No matter how experienced the worship leading team is, they need to rehearse the chorus medleys. Make sure the instrumentalists are playing the right chords. Make sure the drummer knows the correct rhythmic "feel" for each song. Singers should work out simple harmonies during the practice. Devote at least fifteen minutes to chord progressions in different keys and practise improvising instrumental and choral "new songs" to these chord progressions.

4. *Place* If at all possible, practise in the place where the worship service will be. In any event, the worship leading team should meet in the place of worship prior to starting time.

At that time the team leader should confirm the placement of all equipment, instruments and vocalists. The team should rehearse a song-medley while sound engineers check sound levels. Then, after all outward preparation is complete, the team should engage in pre-service prayer together until the service starts.

DUE ORDER TODAY

The contemporary worship leader is the one responsible for the congregation seeking God's Presence according to the due order of "psalms, hymns and spiritual songs." Or, to put this progression into more contemporary terms, the worship should flow from *celebration* to *adoration* to *revelation:*

1. *Psalms* The worship leader should begin the service with "psalmic" celebration. This involves singing Scripture songs exhorting the congregation to offer joyous psalmic sacrifices of praise to the Lord, such as singing, shouting, clapping, lifting hands, dancing, etc. The direction of the lyrics is horizontal — us singing to ourselves ("We Bring the Sacrifice," "Come and Let Us Go," etc.). These song medleys should produce liberty and unity.

2. *Hymns* When the worship leading team has led the congregation into unity and liberty, they should "shift gears" into "hymnic" praise. A hymn (Greek, "humnos") is a song addressed *to* the Lord. Hence, choruses like "I Love You Lord" and "Thou Art Worthy" are technically hymns. The emphasis shifts from celebration to adoration. The lyric direction shifts from horizontal to vertical. The tempo usually shifts from fast to slow. The worship leader may also encourage unaccompanied (a capella) congregational singing to heighten the sense of intimacy with the Lord.

3. *Spiritual Songs* The worship leader should continue in a hymnic mode until that sublime moment when the congregation senses God's manifest Presence. The bridge from

hymns to spiritual songs is the "selah" — instrumental chord progressions that undergird the gentle flow of free congregational worship. During this musical interlude, the worship leading team should be prepared to initiate the Spiritual Song ("ode pneumatica" = God-breathed melody), or Song of the Lord as it was called in Davidic worship. Spiritual songs may begin with an improvised instrumental melody, with accompaniment by other instruments added, followed by choral interpretation by the singers (compare II Chronicles 29:27-28). Often the Song of the Lord is Jesus singing prophetically in the midst of the congregation, a spontaneous "new song" that exhorts, edifies, or encourages the entire congregation.

To summarize, "due order" is the key that releases Spirit-filled worship. This due order necessitates preparation on the part of the worship participants to help them progress in "psalms, hymns and spiritual songs." The result of this preparation and due order is the experiencing of the Presence of Christ as He manifests Himself through prophecy and power.

*The remaining Scriptures quotations in this article are from the **New King James Version,** unless otherwise noted.

CHILDREN
IN WORSHIP
by Arlene Friesen

As anointed music ministries are being raised up in these days to lead the people of God in praise and worship, I believe God's heart is crying out, "Suffer the little ones to come unto Me and forbid them not." *Children, too, can worship the Lord!*

CHILDREN'S NEEDS AND POTENTIAL

God is moving upon children in supernatural ways in our day. We hear of children being saved and filled with the Spirit. We even hear of children being used to minister to adults in various places.

Earlier in this century, for instance, a revival broke out in the midst of a group of poor children, mostly beggars, of the Adullam Rescue Mission in China. In *Visions Beyond the Veil* missionary/author H.A. Baker tells about that Sovereign visitation, a time of prolonged prayer and praise during which remarkable manifestations took place, including genuine conversions, singing in other tongues, visions and revelations of heaven.

Sometimes children's responses to God's presence can teach us adults. In one service we were singing the song "O Lord, You're Beautiful." A handicapped child who was present came forward and knelt in worship. I was told later that people familiar with this child recognized his response in that service as a spiritual barometer reading of the power of God's presence in the place. In that instance that boy was demonstrating an uninhibited and appropriate response to God's presence, one which ministered to the adults around him.

A missionary told me of an occasion when she prayed with a group of five five-to-ten-year-olds, who wanted to be filled with the Spirit. The next evening when they came to the service they asked if they could help pray and as they prayed for adults to receive, those for whom they were praying were "slain in the Spirit!" In another instance, in India, as a group of children were praying for some adults the power of God was so strong that some Hindu people watching them were converted!

Years ago, during one particular family devotion time my oldest brother began to weep over the song "My Jesus, I Love Thee, I Know Thou Art Mine." My parents wondered at this response, but knew God was doing a work. Whether it was then that he accepted Jesus into his heart, my mother doesn't remember, but he did accept the Lord at about age five. Before he went to be with the Lord at age nine he had a deep concern for souls to be saved, including mine. He was the one who shared with me and prayed with me, when I was five, to receive Jesus, too. His sensitivity touched many lives.

In spite of what so often appears to be the case, children's hearts are hungry and longing for the presence of God, for His Spirit and His anointing. They need more than teaching about the truths and stories of the Bible — they need to be saved and baptized in the Holy Spirit. Many need physical and emotional healing, bondages to be broken, to learn to move in the gifts of the Holy Spirit, to overcome the enemy with the Word and to minister to others. In short, in every area within their realm of experience, whether with the adults in a service or apart, children need to be receiving the same dimension of anointed ministry that adults receive in the Lord's house. And just as in the case of adult services, praise and worship and the ministry of music are vital in bringing that anointing. We need to be sowing the seeds God has given us, ministering in faith to our children.

TRAINING RIGHT FROM INFANCY

The Bible gives us some illumination as to the spiritual awareness of young children, even the unborn. John the Baptist was filled with the Spirit from his mother's womb (see Luke 1:15,44). Jeremiah and Paul were set apart for ministry before birth (see Jeremiah 1:5, Galatians 1:15). Timothy was taught the Holy Scriptures from childhood (see II Timothy 3:15 — according to Strong's Concordance, the Greek word for "child" here means "an infant"). Samuel, while still a young child, was recognized throughout Israel as a prophet of God (see I Samuel 3, particularly v. 20). Jesus knew His life's purpose by the time He was twelve (see Luke 2:42,49).

Perhaps we tend to look on examples such as these and other outstanding testimonies, as isolated cases of God's Sovereignty. However, one look at the world system our children are facing today and at the discernment and power they need, is enough to make us cry out *O, that ALL the Lord's people were prophets and that the Lord would put His Spirit upon them!"* (Numbers 11:29)

In recounting the faithfulness of God to His people and the conditions necessary for God's blessings to continue, Moses makes this statement shortly before his death: *"The secret things belong to the Lord our God, but those things which are revealed belong to us AND TO OUR CHILDREN forever, that we may do all the words of this law"* (Deuteronomy 29:29). God's will and purpose is that our children shall not only reap benefits from their parents' obedience and service to the Lord, but shall also be left a legacy, a deposit of spiritual truth and understanding upon which to continue to build the kingdom of God. In other words, as we minister to them what God has given us, they will not have to learn the lessons of the previous generation all over again.

Psalm 78 exhorts us to recount the mighty works of God to succeeding generations so that children yet to be born might also set their hope in the Lord and not be rebellious as their ancestors were. The writer of that psalm, Asaph, is himself a remarkable example of obedience to this command. Appointed as a leading musician in the service of the Tabernacle of David, we find him training his sons in the prophetic music ministry he was appointed to. So effective was the music education program he helped to pioneer that we see descendants of Asaph mentioned in connection with Solomon's Temple and then with the revivals under Kings Jehoshaphat, Hezekiah and Josiah. Even under Ezra and right up until the time of Nehemiah Asaph's offspring were still functioning as musicians, leading praise and worship of the Lord about 500 years after Asaph's time!

GIVING CHILDREN
SUPERNATURAL POWER

One doesn't have to have a special "call" to minister to children, but he does need two things — the anointing and to be a worshipper himself — in order to lead children in worship. We need to be committed to doing more than singing amusing and entertaining songs to hold their attention — though such songs certainly have their place. The children need our help to receive the anointing so that the yoke is broken, for the enemy does all he can to hinder children from entering into God's presence.

What force or strength can a baby or young child have against Satan's power? Babies and children do not appear to us to be spiritually mature enough to do heavy spiritual warfare. In fact, babies seem to be like sponges, totally vulnerable to every influence, unable to resist impressions they are confronted with! We are told, however, in Psalm 8:2 that praise — even in the mouths of infants — silences the enemy. There is a supernatural power released through a child's praise that goes beyond our natural reasoning.

Even though young children's praise often looks like imitations of the adults they respect, Jesus says their praise is perfect (see Matthew 21:15,16). When they praise the Lord they are building a protective shield around their minds and lives, whether they are praising because of our influence or not.

In the ministry organization where I work there is a pre-school nursery for babies through five-year-olds, while their parents attend morning Bible classes. There is ministry in the Word and in praise and worship for these children on a regular basis. Of the five-year-olds who "graduate" after their parents have finished the two-year course, most have been saved and filled with the Spirit.

PRACTICAL MATTERS

As to practical matters in ministering to children, here are some suggestions.

First of all, the worship leader needs to be free to enter into worship himself; he should not be trying to lead worship and correct and discipline the children at the same time! Adult or teen-age helpers can participate with the children, separating the unruly ones if necessary. Also, a good musician at the piano or on guitar is a tremendous aid in maintaining the anointing during quiet worship or during a time of ministering to children individually.

It may help to explain to the children what are appropriate means of expression in praise and worship and why. They must be informed that there are limits: For example, there is freedom to dance, clap our hands and express joy, but not to the degree of foolishness. And tambourines are wonderful for fast songs, but need to be placed under chairs or collected when it's time for "quiet worship." Sometimes a change of order or position is helpful — having the children sit down for quiet worship, for example, or having them come forward and sit on the floor, to diminish the distractions.

There is often need for patient persistence in encouraging the children to enter into singing to the Lord or singing new songs "in the Spirit." We must not give up if it appears the children are uninterested. Sometimes it takes a while for a number of them to respond to the degree that you can sense the atmosphere change. Lack of enthusiastic response is not always an indication that children are not receiving from the Lord. They may surprise us by their response to the Lord later in the service. When the anointing is there and the children are brought to a place of rest in God's presence they may be receiving words that they can share with the rest, so the leader needs to be sensitive to what the Lord is doing.

Anointed music is a wonderful way to minister in the baby nursery as well. Even babies respond to the sound of joyful singing. They become alert and respond with smiles and clapping their hands when happy songs are sung. They are fascinated by visuals with large, colorful objects. Crying babies relax when carried and rocked to the rhythm of songs like "Peace, Peace, Wonderful Peace." Infants and crawlers love to have help in clapping their hands or moving their feet! Toddlers do best if they are made to sit down in one area, with adults behind them, or against a wall. For ages two-five it is good to set their little chairs in a semi-circle and when showing visuals with the songs be sure every child gets a chance to see them up close!

What kind of songs do you use with children? Nursery and pre-school children love illustrated songs. One of my visuals that children enjoyed was to illustrate the song "When My Cup Runneth Over With Joy." I used a pair of "teacup" posters with a happy face on the over-flowing cup and a sad face on the dry cup. Every child related to "happy" and "sad." Actions songs are also good, as they help teach the meaning of songs and provide an outlet for the children's energy.

But children also enjoy the songs of praise and worship used in adult services. Songs with few words and much repetition are best for small children. By our example and word, they too can be taught and encouraged to express their love for Jesus by raising their hands, closing their eyes and singing to the Lord out of their hearts.

A MIGHTY, YOUNG ARMY!

Reaching out to young children in these ways is truly ministering by faith, because one often does not see instant response. Physically, children's growth in ability to sing, as in other areas, develops in stages. We must remember, though, that early musical experiences in an encouraging, positive environment are preparing the child for greater musical awareness and ability later on. Even if the teacher is the only one who is singing, there still is ministry taking place in the life of the child.

Recently I was told about God's moving upon the children at the International Worship Symposium in Bogota, Colombia. The sister in charge of the children's ministry there reported that on the first day, children were saved, filled with the Spirit and "slain" under the power of God. The second day God took over in the worship as children received prophecies, were called into ministry and were given gifts from the Lord. On the last day the children formed a worship procession in the adults' service. As the singers who were dressed as soldiers formed an arch with their swords, the others came through — first the banners, then the dancers, then the instruments (tambourines, flutes and rhythm instruments) and finally, the puppets. With the adult orchestra providing the accompaniment, the congregation was moved to praise, worship and brokenness before the Lord at this display.

God has a special destiny for our children, not just after they're grown up, but now! He is placing a burden on our hearts to equip them to stand against the enemy in this day and to lead their peers and adults into the kingdom of God. He wants a whole generation of little John the Baptists, Jeremiahs, Samuels, Davids and Timothys — a mighty army of young worshippers, warriors and workers for God!

PRAISE
IN THE HOME
by Andrew Picklyk

What we do corporately as a church should affect our total daily life-style. If not, church becomes a form and ritual devoid of reality and power. This is exactly the case in regard to praise. God has given a real renewal of praise in the church and there are many excellent and necessary seminars to bring congregations into glorious praise. Yet there is a limited amount of time spent to initiate and enhance praise in the home.

I am not suggesting a program where we stand in rows at home and have a worship leader conduct a praise session. More important than that kind of thing is to have praise worked right into the fabric of our lives. Could we not develop a spirit of praise in our home, one that will permeate every aspect of the life of each member of the family? How would this spirit of praise better our lives and how can we develop it in our home?

Praise in the home should keep our focus consistently on God as our total Source. Such acknowledgment prevents us from the sin of self-sufficiency and pride. The concept of the home and the way it functions is sourced in God. The family's understanding should be that the home does not function according to the ideas of the family members; rather each one is to recognize the Lord as the final Authority. If praise is not functioning in the home, God will not likely be recognized in this way, which means that conflict arises as to whose idea or way is better. When Jesus is centralized, however, by the family consistently praising Him, such conflicts are overcome.

A spirit of praise will also create a positive atmosphere in the home. Atmosphere is as important to a good home as climate is to growing fruit. When the prophet needed a word from God, he called on the praising minstrel to create an atmosphere for the prophetic (see II Kings 3:11-15). When Saul needed relief from demonic oppression, he did the same (see I Samuel 16:17,23). Praising God has the creative power to dispel the negative and replace it with the positive.

Praise in the home will create an attitude of appreciation and thanksgiving. We begin to see the good in each other and compliment it, which strengthens our relationships with one another. This is another way praise helps create a positive atmosphere in which faith can function more effectively. The Bible says that if a husband and wife aren't getting along well, their prayers are frustrated or hindered (see I Peter 3:7).

The greatest accomplishment of praise in the home is the way it enhances the presence of God. God inhabits the praises of His people (Psalm 22:3) and in His presence is fulness of joy (Psalm 16:11). By the active presence of the Spirit of God all good, spiritual fruit is produced (Galatians 5:22-23) and every family needs the fruit of the Spirit.

How can I bring praise and all its benefits into my home?

1. Start with you and the Lord alone. Repent of an unthankful, negative attitude. Exercise the spirit of praise in your private life. Think on good and positive things. Daily count up all the blessings of the Lord. Rejoice in Christ's goodness to you. Determine to make every effort, with God's help, to be thankful for all things.

2. Bring this personal renewal of thanksgiving and praise into your family devotions. Praise God for one another and acknowledge the work of God in each one's life. Also, share the blessings of God with the family. If our prayers get too "need-centered" we seemingly dwarf the majesty of God. In such cases faith wavers. Reflect more on Who God is than what our needs are. Songs of praise are very effective in this regard.

3. Praise also needs to be integrated with our regular, daily activities. The Bible says that at all times we are to permeate our activities with loving God (Deuteronomy 6:5-9). As we walk, talk, fellowship, etc., praise to God must be a priority ingredient. All our works, great and small, should honour our Lord.

Whatever is to be successful needs to be done in an atmosphere that breeds success. In the home praise can become a fundamental desire that springs from our inner man, a habit that influences our attitudes, guides our speech, beautifies our actions and enriches all relationships.

14

SUPPORTIVE MUSIC MINISTERS
by Dwight Greiner

God's Word is a book of patterns — patterns which God repeatedly exhorts His servants to follow (see Exodus 25:40; Hebrews 8:5; I Chronicles 28:11-12, 19-20; etc.). Just as there are patterns for church government, the operation of spiritual gifts, evangelism, etc., there is also a pattern for praise and worship and a pattern for team ministry. These latter two are intertwined to give multiplied strength to the work of God. By examining them we will see what a key function musicians have in helping the church follow the overall Biblical pattern, so that it accomplishes its spiritual goals.

An important aspect of the pattern for choosing leaders in God's house is to *"know them which labour among you..."* (I Thessalonians 5:12). God's pattern for choosing leaders is based on this "proving principle" (see also I Timothy 3:10; I Thessalonians 5:21) or in other words, choice is made on

111

the basis of the candidate's track record. Have they been faithful in attendance and tithing? Do they demonstrate the surrendered life and the servant spirit? Are they teachable and sensitive to the voice of God?

The character and life-style of the musician are perhaps even more important than his skill and ability. It has been disappointing over the years to see individuals with tremendous abilities not reach their potential due to flaws and inconsistencies in their character which they refused to acknowledge and deal with. Godly character qualities are like pillars that hold up the gift or ministry. If weaknesses or flaws in the character are not overcome, it can mean the collapse and failure of one's ministry. However, when a person is chosen for an area of ministry according to the pattern of God's Word, it eliminates a lot of heartache and hurt. We recognize that there is never a guarantee that a person won't have problems, but we are always wise to make choices in accordance with God's Word.

Because their ministry puts them before people, musicians are vulnerable to pride and the praise of men. Satan or Lucifer was at one time the chief musician or worship leader in heaven, but became proud and jealous of God's glory and was cast down from his place of ministry. Those in supportive music ministry must die daily to the flesh and must wait submissively on God to determine His will and direction.

Those who minister in the area of music are key people in strengthening the ministry of those who share the Word of God. It is a refreshing and edifying experience to be in a service where the worship leader has the anointing of God upon him and leads with obvious sensitivity to the direction of the Holy Spirit. When this occurs your heart is brought into communion with the Lord and is prepared for the ministry of the Word. On the other hand, if those who lead in worship are not prepared in spirit they are apt to be insensitive to the leading of the Holy Spirit and cause the meeting to miss the mark. This can make it very difficult for those who share the Word, for hearts have not been prepared to receive through meaningful participation in praise and worship.

It is essential that there be a tremendous unity between the worship leader and the rest of the ministry team. An effective worship leader will be particularly sensitive to the senior pastor and the direction God is giving him. Worship leading is not the place for the person who is independent and wanting to do his own thing. In Psalm 133 we are told that unity and the anointing are interdependent; where His people are in unity, God commands His blessing. There was unity in the upper room when the disciples were there in one accord on the day of Pentecost (Acts 2) and then again some days later when they were praying and praising and the Holy Spirit moved again (Acts 4:23-32). These are just two examples of the Holy Spirit being poured out in response to unity.

I would like to leave you with some principles taken from a worship leader's guide published by Bible Temple in Portland, Oregon, U.S.A., which I found to be very practical and helpful.

PRINCIPLES OF LEADING WORSHIP

1. Spend time before the service in prayer and preparation. Obey the leading of the Spirit. Ask those in leadership how long they desire to sing. Step to the pulpit unassuming.

2. Be relaxed, smile, dress properly and show genuine enthusiasm. You are to inspire the people and help them to take their minds off themselves and put them upon Christ.

3. Announce songs clearly. Repeat location. Know the key and use mikes to help lead when changing choruses without stopping. What you do, they will do (clap, lift hands, dance, etc.).

4. Don't be a choppy leader (fast, slow, fast). Several songs

with the same theme, key and tempo will move the people into unity and the flow of the Spirit. Unless the Lord directs otherwise, start service with faster songs, then move into slower worship songs.

5. Don't make people stand unnecessarily long. You may alternate standing and sitting times.

6. Don't scold the people. It most always has a negative reaction. Inspire by exhortation, as the Lord directs, but don't preach between songs or down at them. Avoid idle words.

7. After strong worship — wait — don't move too fast — silence is not harmful. Let God minister.

8. Know when to quit! The best time is at the spiritual peak of the service. Silently step back from the pulpit, yielding it for the next leader.

9. Remember, obey the Holy Spirit. Every service is different. (II Chronicles 29:30)

Music plays a key role in every move of God and the present one is no exception. All these and many more areas are being illuminated and emphasized in a fresh, new way in our day. As music ministers commit themselves to God's pattern for them, the music ministry of the church will continue to be a major builder of the present move.

SPIRITUAL
SONGS
by David K. Blomgren

The New Testament clearly exhorts that there are to be three forms of singing found regularly in the house of the Lord. Ephesians 5:18b-19 states, *"be filled with the Spirit; Speaking to yourselves in psalms and hymns and spiritual songs, singing and making melody in your heart to the Lord."* One of the characteristics of being Spirit-filled is that the believer will sing unto the Lord. He will sing in psalms, hymns and spiritual songs. So also Colossians 3:16 confirms, *"Let the word of Christ dwell in you richly in all wisdom; teaching and admonishing one another in psalms and hymns and spiritual songs, singing with grace in your hearts to the Lord."*

The singing of "Psalms" is basically the singing of Scripture. It is Scriptural passages put to a new melody. The usage of the Greek term, *psalmos*, clearly refers to more than just the Old Testament book of Psalms.

"Hymns" are songs of praise of human composition by various hymn writers on different Christian themes. Thousands of beautiful hymns have been composed over the centuries and have been sung in countless churches.

"Spiritual songs" are songs of a spontaneous or unpremeditated nature, sung under the impetus of the Holy Spirit. They are "new songs", never sung before. This fulfils the command of Psalm 96:1, *"O sing unto the Lord a new song: sing unto the Lord, all the earth."* (See also Psalm 98:1.) New songs are the worship of Heaven (see Revelation 5:8-9).

TYPES OF
SPIRITUAL SONGS

There are two types of spiritual songs. They are described prophetically by Jeremiah as to be operative in the last days. Jeremiah predicted that the day would come when the voices of the Bride and the Bridegroom would be heard, *"the voice of joy and the voice of gladness, the voice of the bridegroom and the voice of the bride, the voice of them that shall say, Praise the Lord of hosts: for the Lord is good; for his mercy endureth for ever..."* (Jeremiah 33:11). These two types of spiritual songs are:

1) *The Song of Praise (sung primarily to God):* This is a new song of praise sung to the Lord. It is a love song of the Bride to the Bridegroom. As the Bridegroom exhorts the Bride to sing to Him, she responds in new song, *"The flowers appear on the earth; the time of the singing...is come...let me hear thy voice; for sweet is thy voice"* (Song of Solomon 2:12,14). It is a song *to* the Lord;

2) *The Song of the Lord (sung primarily to others under the direction of the Holy Spirit):* This is a new song from the Lord sung through a yielded vessel. It is a prophetic song from the Bridegroom to the Bride. It is a song *of* the Lord. The writer of Hebrews indicated that Jesus, the Bridegroom,

would be singing in the midst of His church: "I will declare thy name unto my brethren, in the midst of the church will I sing praise unto thee" (Hebrews 2:12). The Song of the Lord as it is operative today, also fulfils the prophecy of Zephaniah, *"The Lord thy God in the midst of thee is mighty...He will joy over thee with singing"* (Zephaniah 3:17).

PREPARATION TO SING SPIRITUAL SONGS

Preparation is a Godly principle. The Lord is desirous that there be a "holy priesthood" who come before Him, lifting up "holy hands" (see I Peter 2:5; I Timothy 2:8). They come acceptably before the Lord, as instructed in Psalm 24:3b-4: *"who shall stand in his holy place? He that hath clean hands and a pure heart."*

In the Old Testament we see that those who came in as priests to minister to God had to prepare themselves before they ministered in the Holy Place. There were four areas of preparation according to Exodus 28:41-42. They were the following:

1) *Anointed:* They were to be anointed with the holy anointing oil. In the same manner today, the royal priesthood must be anointed by the Holy Spirit.

2) *Consecrated by Cleansing:* This cleansing took place at the brazen laver. There they washed their feet, symbolic of the cleansing of their walk and washed their hands, symbolic of the cleansing of their deeds (see Exodus 30:18-21). The Hebrew word for "consecration", *mala yad,* literally means "to fill the hands". The implication is that the priest could not have his hands filled with an acceptable sacrifice to God without this preparation.

3) *Set Aside to Service:* This refers to the sanctifying process whereby blood was applied to the ear (set aside to hear), to the thumb of the right hand (set aside to do) and to the great

117

toe of the right foot (set aside to walk properly) (see Exodus 29:20).

4) *Properly Garbed:* This refers to the putting on of the linen breeches which covered the priest's nakedness. This is fulfilled in our being properly garbed in the garments of praise (see Isaiah 61:3).

There was a great number of ceremonies they had to abide by for cleanliness. A person was considered defiled if he came into contact with unclean things. They were defiled by contact with the carcass of an unclean animal, or contact with a dead person (see Leviticus 11:24; Numbers 19:17-22). If a bug crawled across his hand, that priest was unclean. These ceremonies which were external were as a picture book that illustrated what God wants on the inside.

Furthermore, the preparation to sing spiritual songs should include the following:

5) *A life wholly dedicated to God:* II Chronicles 29:27 states, *"When the burnt offering began, the song of the Lord began also..."* The burnt offering was an offering dedicated wholly to the Lord. Nothing was to be held back, but everything was to be given to God as His portion. When this is done spiritually, the Song of the Lord will begin.

6) *Wait on One's Ministry:* The singers and musicians were to "wait" on their ministry (see II Chronicles 7:6; 13:10).

DEFINITION OF
SPIRITUAL SONGS

The Song of Praise as a "new" song involves four elements:

1) *A Love Song:* An expression of love from the Bride;

2) *A Song of Exaltation of God:* This expression acknowledges the worthiness of God and is an acknowledgment of what He has done (see Revelation 5:9; Psalm 150:2);

3) *A Song of Seeking the Lord:* This song expresses a desire to draw closer to the Lord;

4) *A Song of Thanksgiving:* This song is an expression of our gratitude to God.

The Song of the Lord as a "new" song involves four elements:

1) *A Word of Prophecy in Song:* This song warns and gives direction according to Scriptural principles;

2) *A Word of Encouragement in Song:* This word comes to lift spirits;

3) *A Word of Exhortation in Song:* This word in song comes to shake us to action and to do the Lord's bidding;

4) *A Word of Comfort in Song:* This song may come in times of trials or difficulties. It is a healing balm and is a comforting, soothing word to a wound.

OPERATION OF SPIRITUAL SONGS

The following are some guidelines for the operation of spiritual songs in the assembly of God's people:

1) When singing a spiritual song, do it clearly and loud enough so that everyone can hear;

2) Don't draw attention to yourself by being too loud;

3) Try to stay on key, if possible. If you cannot stay on key, don't sing it; just prophesy it!

4) Watch the length of your song. This time is not intended to be a spiritual opera. Leave the "everlasting" songs for Heaven;

5) The message given in the song should stay in the same vein the Holy Spirit has already indicated in the service;

6) Be sensitive that your song's tempo does not break the atmosphere already present in the service. If the prophetic flow of the service is one of victory and joy, then a slow, sombre song would be out of place and would break that thrust of the Spirit;

7) There should not be any mannerisms or exhibitionism which would draw the attention of the people to yourself and away from the Lord.

God is restoring the singing of spiritual songs to His house today. David cried, *"Compass me about with songs of deliverance."* Let us all believe that God will fill each house of God so that it is encompassed about with new songs, songs of deliverance, songs of victory and songs of the Lord.

PART IV

GOD'S DESIRE
FOR PRAISE & WORSHIP

THE SPIRIT
OF WORSHIP
by Mike Herron

Worship is one of the most vital activities of the church. Sincere worship delights the heart of God, refreshes the soul of man and releases the presence and power of God to His people. Insincere worship leaves the church centered on man and his abilities and therefore results in lifeless form and meaningless repetition.

"...must worship Him in Spirit..." is the requirement of Jesus in John 4:24. What did He mean by that statement?

WHAT IS WORSHIP IN SPIRIT?

A.W. Tozer gave an appropriate answer to this question in his book *Worship: The Missing Jewel in the Evangelical Church.* He pointed out three elements of true, heartfelt worship.

1) "You must 'feel' in the heart." We are drifting away from emotional expressions in the church. We are in danger of being infiltrated with the spirit of this age which depicts man as rational, unemotional and above all, governed by his intellectual abilities. Paul states that *"with the heart man believes..."* (Romans 10:10, NASB). The emotional center of man must become involved in true worship.

2) "A humbling but delightful sense of admiring awe and astonishing wonder." When people stand at the banks of the Grand Canyon for the first time, they are filled with a sense of astonishment at the immensity of God's creation. An even greater sense of wonderment should fill the believer's heart when he consciously turns his thoughts toward the Creator/ Saviour. Our sense of awe will increase as we meditate and pray over the awesomeness of God's great act of redemption through Jesus Christ our Lord. In Revelation 4:11 the Lord is worshipped as Creator: *"You are worthy, our Lord and God...for you created all things..."* (NIV). In Revelation 5:9, the Lamb is worshipped as the Redeemer: *"And they sang a new song: 'You are worthy...because you were slain and with your blood you purchased men for God..."* (NIV).

WORSHIPPER OR WORKER?

In Luke 10:38-42 we have the two extremes of Christians represented in the personalities of Martha and Mary. Martha was "cumbered," "careful," and "troubled." Mary was "collected" as she sat at Jesus' feet. She was "carefree" as she put every temporal thought from her mind to eat of His words and "triumphant" as she gained everlasting insights from the Lord.

One lesson we should learn from this story is that our worship time is a time to put aside EVERY TEMPORAL THOUGHT and concentrate totally on the Person of Jesus. It is time to cease from being a worker and be completely a worshipper! Let the problems arise, let the dishes sit in the sink, let the crumbs lie on the floor; it is time to SIT AT HIS FEET! This is not a matter of irresponsibility or of an unrealistic attitude toward life, but one of disciplining your mind to concentrate on God. And then the joys of beholding Jesus will naturally begin flowing from your heart. *"Those who look to him are radiant; their faces are never covered with shame"* (Psalm 34:5, NIV).

There is a unique formula for worship and service in the Scripture. In Deuteronomy 8:19 we are given the formula for *service* and *worship: "If thou do at all forget the Lord thy God and walk after other gods and SERVE them and WORSHIP them...ye shall surely perish."*

In a very real sense, what we serve is what we worship. As servants of the Lord we are constantly in danger of putting *service* ahead of *worship,* and we begin to reap the subsequent rewards promised in this verse — "You will perish!" Without the renewing discipline of worship with its benefit of fresh inspiration, we begin a process of spiritual "perishing" or slow decay.

Jesus gave us the answer to this problem in Luke 4:8 where He stated *"It is written: 'WORSHIP the Lord your God and SERVE him only' "* (NIV). Putting *worship* ahead of *service* is hard for us to do because man tends to measure his self worth by outward accomplishments. God, on the other hand, ponders the motives of the heart.

Worship and then *service* becomes a spiritual antidote to Satanic temptation and harassment, as seen in verse 13 of Luke 4. *"When the devil had finished all this tempting, he left Him..."* (NIV). It is hard to knock a "true worshipper" off the track, because he loves the Lord with all his heart, his soul, his strength and his mind (see Mark 12:30). The true worshipper is serving God totally, because he is worshipping with the totality of his being!

NEW TESTAMENT CONCEPTS
OF WORSHIP

There are four different words in the Greek language that

are translated into the English word "worship." Each word holds a key to a true understanding of worship in Spirit and truth.

1) Proskuneo: In Luke 7:36-50 the woman with the alabaster box displays the meaning of this word — *"to make obeisance, do reverence, to kiss."* The Pharisee gave Jesus meat (v. 36), but no love or worship! In contrast, the woman in this account exhibited five basic elements of one who worships Jesus in spirit and truth:

a) Emotions: Luke 7:38 says she *"stood at his feet behind him weeping..."* I am not advocating an emotional church, full of sentimentality, but this woman honestly loved Him so much that SHE COULDN'T CONTAIN HER FEELINGS! If you have never had the depths of your soul touched by the love of God it is time to pray until the fountains of the deep are broken up. Rivers of living water are supposed to be flowing from within the believer's belly. How many people do you know who could have a river flowing through their inwards and not feel it? Laughter, weeping, joy, fear — these are all valid, emotional responses to the various manifestations of God's presence.

b) Substance: The alabaster box of ointment in verse 37 represents something of great cost to the worshipper. Alabaster is formed by a slow process of water distilling into stalactites and stalagmites in caves and crevices around springs. The ointment is made by a slow process of crushing, drying and mixing. Worship is a process that involves our most precious commodity — time! It is precious and costly to worship God.

c) Service: Sincere worship will foster an unquenchable desire to serve both God and our fellow man. In verse 38 the woman washed Jesus' feet with her tears, the action of the lowliest servant of all. Could a lack of Christian service in the church today be connected with a lack of revelation of what true worship of Christ is?

124

d) Honour: In I Corinthians 1:15 we are told that a woman's long hair is *"a glory to her..."* Yet this woman willingly subjugated her greatest source of pride and truly *"put all things under his feet"* (Psalm 8:6) by washing Jesus' feet with her hair. Isaac Watts captured her feelings in the second stanza of his famous hymn, "When I Survey the Wondrous Cross":

> Forbid it, Lord, that I should boast,
> save in the death of Christ my God;
> All the vain things that charm me most —
> I sacrifice them to His blood.

e) Love: She ceased not to kiss Jesus' feet for the duration of His visit to the Pharisee's home (v. 45). Jesus interpreted her actions in verse 47 when He said, *"she LOVED much..."* Love must be expressed in action to be transformed from the realm of the theoretical into the practical. Worship is a time to express our love to Jesus by wholehearted singing, praise, lifting of hands and other manifestations mentioned in God's songbook, the Psalms. In Psalm 2:12 we are told to *"Kiss the Son, lest he be angry and ye perish from the way, when his wrath is kindled but a little..."* The Pharisee fell under the curse of these words when he failed to acknowledge the Son of God with a kiss of love and appreciation. Without worship, he began the process of "perishing from the way." The proud can never worship God in a Biblical manner; it is reserved for the lowly of heart!

2) Sebomai: This Greek word for worship is found in Matthew 15:9. Jesus condemns this form of worship in His statement, *"But in vain they do worship me, teaching for doctrines the commandments of men."* The vanity or emptiness that the Lord refers to is found in the very meaning of sebomai — "To revere a deity with no action."

In all New Testament references to valid worship, the word used is a *verb*, not a *noun*! Worship is not a thing, it is something that one does, a definable act that distinguishes him from the

125

crowd. The three Hebrew children in Daniel 3 would not participate in the actions of worship and thus sealed their destiny in
the fiery furnace. True worshippers are identified by what they
do, not just the intentions or thoughts of their hearts!

3) Sebazomai: The third word for our study means "to
honour religiously." A true worshipper will be a regular, consis-
tent admirer of the Lord Jesus Christ and will carry in his heart
a sense of duty to unceasingly worship the true God. This word
is used in the negative sense in Romans 1:25: *"They exchanged
the truth of God for a lie and worshipped and served created
things rather than the Creator..."* (NIV). The results of refusing
to worship the Lord are alarming and should cause us to search
our hearts and respond to the Spirit's call to worship.

Romans 1:21 describes this refusal to worship as consisting
of two things: (i) *"they neither glorified him as God...,"* (ii) *"nor
gave thanks to him..."* (NIV). It was not a problem of knowing
or acknowledging God, but of glorifying Him in worship.

Thanksgiving is the sinew and fibre of worship.

When faithfulness in worship was misdirected, there began
the "perishing process" that resulted in the fulfilment of unrighteousness (vv. 29-32): fornication, wickedness, covetousness,
maliciousness, etc.

The mind also undergoes a degenerative process when true
worship is refused: *"their thinking became futile and their foolish
hearts were darkened"* (v. 21, NIV). And finally they were left
with a *"depraved mind..."* (v. 28, NIV), void of the knowledge
of God, the ultimate depth of degeneration.

4) Ethelothreskeia: Our last word is "worship one prescribes
for himself." In Colossians 2:16-23 (NIV) we find three manifestations of this form of worship.

a) *Exterior Worship* (Colossians 2:16,17): Here Paul con-
trasts the natural, exterior observances of the Levitical laws as
being an unacceptable shadow of worship, which shadow is
pointing to the reality of Christ. *"Do not let anyone judge you*

by what you eat or drink, or with regard to a religious festival, a New Moon celebration or a Sabbath day. These are a shadow of the things that were to come; the reality, however, is found in Christ." WORSHIP IS TO FOCUS ON THE PERSON OF CHRIST, NOT ON A PERFORMANCE!

b) *Angelic Worship* (Colossians 2:18): Paul discredits this mistaken form of spirituality by the statement *"Do not let anyone who delights in false humility and the worship of angels disqualify you for the prize."* WORSHIP IS CENTERED ON THE PRE-EMINENCE OF CHRIST, NOT SPIRITUAL MANIFESTATIONS!

c) *Humanistic Worship* (Colossians 2:22-23): Worship that is based on human commands and teachings is also discredited as being of no benefit to the true believer. *"Such regulations indeed have an appearance of wisdom, with their self-imposed worship...but they lack any value..."*

Clearly we see from this verse that WORSHIP IS CENTERED ON THE *PRESENCE* OF CHRIST, NOT THE RITUALS OF MAN!

CHARACTERISTICS OF THE SPIRIT OF WORSHIP

1) Rejoicing and joy: The spirit of worship is well-described in the narrative of the wise men from the east (see Matthew 2:10-11). *"When they saw the star, they rejoiced with exceeding great joy"* (v. 10). Worship is not exclusively solemn, heavy and serious. It is the ultimate of joy! *"In thy presence is fulness of joy; at thy right hand there are pleasures for evermore"* (Psalm 16:11). Worship is designed to strengthen the body of Christ through the joy of the Lord! (Compare Nehemiah 8:10.)

In Revelation 19:4 we see worship: *"the four and twenty elders and the four beasts fell down and WORSHIPPED God..."* In verse 5 we see praise: *"PRAISE our God, all ye his servants and ye that fear him, both small and great."* In verse 7 we see

127

the joy of the Lord: "Let us be GLAD and REJOICE and give honour to him..." These three, like the Father, Son and Holy Spirit are inseparable yet distinct in their own attributes.

2) Revelation of Christ: "And when they were come into the HOUSE they SAW the young child with Mary his mother..." (Matthew 2:11). The house of the Lord is the place where God unveils Himself to us. *"To see thy power and thy glory, so as I HAVE SEEN THEE IN THE SANCTUARY"* (Psalm 63:2). When we gather together as God's house, we should be able to say with Isaiah, *"I saw also the Lord sitting upon the throne, high and lifted up and his train filled the temple"* (IIsaiah 6:1). Worship brings greater reality to the things of God.

3) Falling down: "They saw...and fell down and worshipped him..." (Matthew 2:11). The place of worship throughout the Scripture is at the feet of Christ, fulfilling God's unchangeable decree in Ephesians 1:22, "(God) *hath put all things under his feet and gave Him to be the head over all things to the church."* In worship we put ourselves in our rightful place — at the feet of Jesus — but we are not beneath them, for that is the place reserved for His enemies!

THE PROPHETIC SPIRIT IN WORSHIP
by Dr. David K. Blomgren

Worship unto God is not only a duty for the redeemed; it is also a pleasure. However, worship can become mechanical and dry if we do it as a form or a habit and not with a rejoicing heart of pleasure in the Lord.

There is a realm of prophetic unction which brings a dimension of Divine quickening into our worship. When the Holy Spirit moves in a service in response to the high worship of God's people, a prophetic spirit of anointing may come upon the congregation. This spirit of prophetic anointing comes as a mantle upon the corporate people of God, quickening life, anointing the prophetic voice, causing the gifts of the Spirit to flow and bringing conviction to the sinner and healing to the hurting.

This realm of prophetic unction is mentioned in Revelation 19:10b: *"Worship God: for the testimony of Jesus is the spirit of prophecy."* The prophetic spirit coming and permeating the worship atmosphere is a witness of the presence of Jesus being manifest in the service.

QUICKENING THE PROPHETIC SPIRIT

When God's people worship intensely *"in spirit and in truth"* (John 4:24), there is birthed by God a prophetic spirit in the worship. In II Kings 3:11-16 the prophet Elisha is approached by Jehoshaphat to bring a prophetic word regarding Judah's dilemma. Elisha understood that true worship brings the prophetic spirit. So he gave the instruction, *"Now bring me a minstrel. And it came to pass, when the minstrel played, that the hand of the Lord came upon him. And he said, Thus saith the Lord..."* (vv. 15-16). The minstrel began to sing new songs of praise unto the Lord. Doubtless, as the minstrel played new songs, Elisha also lifted his voice in praise until the prophetic spirit fell upon him and he began to prophesy.

Another example is that of the company of prophets in I Samuel 10:5-10. The prophet Samuel, who initiated the School of the Prophets, understood clearly what births the prophetic spirit. Samuel tells Saul that a company of prophets will be coming down the road to function in the prophetic ministry, playing songs of praise on musical instruments of pipes, harps and tabrets, worshipping and birthing the prophetic spirit. Eusebius, the father of church history (third century A.D.) tells us that the instruction of the school of the prophets included systematic and thorough music education (*Praeparatic Evangelica*, xi:5). Samuel's word was that the prophetic spirit would come with such power that even Saul would prophesy and by the power of the prophetic anointing Saul would *"be turned into another man"* (I Samuel 10:6b).

Likewise today, when a prophetic spirit is upon a congregation, anyone who exercises faith could prophesy. I Corinthians 14:31 states, *"For ye may all prophesy one by one..."* Those who do not have the gift of prophecy and who are not prophets cannot prophesy except when there is a strong spirit of prophecy upon them. The spirit of prophecy enables them to prophesy the word of the Lord, without which occasion of special endowment they could not prophesy. Moses was willing that all the Lord's people would prophesy (see Numbers 11:29). Consequently the 70 elders of Israel all prophesied under the anointing. In I Samuel 19:20-24 Saul sent three different groups of messengers, who could not otherwise prophesy, to a company of prophets. The result was that they all prophesied when they came under the prophetic spirit.

It is not God's purpose for everyone to prophesy in any one service. Rather, let it be noted that anyone *can* minister in the prophetic spirit when the prophetic unction rests upon the corporate gathering. Thus we may conclude that the singers and worshippers are responsible to birth the prophetic spirit through their worship.

THE PROPHETIC BURDEN

We clearly see the prophetic spirit in Davidic worship. King David was a sweet psalmist and as he would lift his voice in new songs of praise in accompaniment to the harp, the prophetic spirit would anoint him.

David brought the Ark of the Covenant, representing God's presence and placed it in a tent known as the Tabernacle of David on Mount Zion. There he appointed Levitical priests to play on instruments and sing *"to minister before the ark of the Lord and to record and to thank and praise the Lord God of Israel"* (I Chronicles 16:4).

David appointed a man named Chenaniah as head of the appointed singers and worshippers in the Tabernacle of David. He is described as *"the master of the song"* (KJV) in I Chronicles 15:27. This phrase in the Hebrew is *hasar hammasa,* meaning literally, "The prince of bearing the *burden.*" This word

131

"burden" (Hebrew, *massa*) is used elsewhere in Scripture as a technical term of the prophetic burden of the prophets. Several examples will illustrate this.

Habakkuk 1:1 states, *"The BURDEN* (Hebrew, *massa*) *which Habakkuk the prophet did see";* Malachi 1:1, *"The BURDEN* (Hebrew, *massa*) of *the word of the Lord to Israel by Malachi";* Nahum 1:1, *"The BURDEN* (Hebrew, *massa*) of *Nineveh. The book of the vision of Nahum..."*

The word in this sense had the concept of "carrying" in grave responsibility the prophetic spirit as a heavy weight. The singers and worshippers are responsible to bear the prophetic burden, to bring it into the corporate gathering.

Musicians need to understand that God is restoring to them a powerful but awesome responsibility that has not been understood in former days. Musicians have often been like performers, caught up with their music as an art. But God is doing a new thing today. God is raising up musicians who are skillful and above all have the Davidic spirit of prophetic anointing. They are not only performers but true worshippers.

The musicians in the Tabernacle of David and the Temple of Solomon were to take the lead in bearing the burden of the prophetic spirit. The prophetic spirit of the Levitical singers caused them to compose by the Spirit psalms to be sung, such as those by Asaph, Heman and others. The musician operated to prophesy on the instrument or in vocal song (see I Chronicles 25:1-2).

The Hebrew word to "prophesy" *(naba)* means "to bubble up, to gush forth, to pour out." This describes the human activity of the prophetic spirit in response to the anointing of God upon the musician and worshipper. Thus the prophetic spirit pours forth from him in new song or prophetic ministry like water from a fountain.

The Levitical musicians were called "seers" (I Chronicles 25:5). The word "seer" (Hebrew, *chozeh*) denotes the receptive mode of "seeing" a message from God in the prophetic spirit. The level of prophetic revelation is always parallel to the level of worship through the musicians and worshippers in a service.

Therefore musicians have a grave responsibility to "wait" on their ministry (see II Chronicles 7:6; 13:10). To "wait" (Hebrew, *math*) meant literally "to stand" in the sense of standing to wait for orders and direction so that one might serve a king. The concept is similar to a waiter who "waits" on a table for directions as to the menu. Musicians and all worshippers must "wait" on the Lord, standing in His presence before a service to know the direction from the Lord of spiritual ministry in the prophetic spirit.

The word for the prophetic burden (Hebrew, *massa*) etymologically has the meaning of "lifting up." It is used in Ezekiel 24:25 (*"that whereupon they set their minds";* to describe the lifting up of the soul in the prophetic spirit by the temple musicians. The ministry of the musician through worship must sometimes lift his own soul so that he may lift up the soul of others. Thus David cried, *"Unto thee, O Lord, do I LIFT up* (Hebrew, *massa*) *my soul"* (Psalm 25:1). See also Psalm 86:4; 143:8.

INSTRUCTION IN THE
PROPHETIC SPIRIT

Chenaniah *"instructed about the song..."* (I Chronicles 15:22). The word "song" in both cases in this verse is this same Hebrew word (*massa* or *hammasa*) as used for the prophetic burden. Chenaniah was skillful in the prophetic anointing and instructed others how to birth the prophetic spirit and flow in new prophetic songs. We need to instruct, with systematic teaching, the musicians as well as the congregation, so that they understand how to operate in that anointing to the lifting up of God's people.

They would be instructed to respond to the power of the

prophetic spirit to defeat the enemy. In II Chronicles 20:14-19 we see a temple musician, Jahaziel, on whom the prophetic spirit comes in the midst of the temple worship. He prophesies that God will give a great victory to His people. Musicians and singers are then placed before the army to praise the Lord and by their worship the enemy is ambushed.

They would be instructed how David played on his harp when King Saul was tormented by oppressive, evil spirits. The prophetic spirit of David's worship caused the evil spirits to flee and Saul was refreshed (see I Samuel 16:14-23).

They would be instructed to minister in the prophetic spirit on the instruments, playing new songs with the prophetic unction (see I Chronicles 25:1-2), learning to flow in the tempo and the timing of what God would say to speak to His people.

The presence of Jesus and the witness of His presence in the prophetic spirit in our worship is not an option. We must have the prophetic anointing of God in our corporate worship. The time has now come that Jesus spoke about when He said, *"the hour cometh and now is, when the true worshippers shall worship the Father in spirit and in truth: for the Father seeketh such to worship him"* (John 4:23).

FROM PRAISE TO WORSHIP
by Dr. Howard Rachinski

My earliest recollections of church life consist of hours and hours and HOURS of praising the Lord. I remember vividly those pre- and post-service prayer meetings of my childhood, when my thoughts would drift dreamily away to baseball, football, planning next week's playtime activities, pondering my wish list ("If I had a million dollars..."), etc. Suddenly my euphoric state would be soundly interrupted by the commanding voice of my pastor, "Come on son, let's praise the Lord." His emphatic "suggestion" would then be supported by direct physical implementation. He would reach down, lift up my hands and begin to praise the Lord for me. I would then quickly join him in this "flow" realizing that the sooner I got with it, the sooner he would go on to another unsuspecting child. Sometimes it worked, sometimes it didn't...

Other comatose moments were disturbed instantly by the

awareness of my father's penetrating stare. Dad didn't have to say anything; I *KNEW* what he meant! Without hesitation I would lift my hands up and praise the Lord as loud and as fervently as possible.

During those obedient times, with all the blood rushing out of my upraised hands to crowd into the rest of my body, I began to wonder if I would survive my childhood. Because our prayer and worship times would last an hour, I was sure rigor mortis had entered my arms permanently. Incredible panic would set in as I underwent this agonizing physical torture — I would never be able to pick up a bat or throw a ball again! But my fear of the authoritative figures in my life far outweighed my fear of physical demise.

Now, before there are gasps of shock and dismay and before I am besieged with outcries of child abuse, unfair legalistic harassment, etc., allow me to qualify my recollections. I not only look back to my childhood with the fondest of memories, but also with the greatest sense of appreciation for such a Divine heritage. I consider myself as very blessed to have grown up under the ministry of Pastor Reg Layzell, whom some called an "apostle of praise." When I reflect back on the truths that were grounded in me as a child and observe the fresh awakening that is occurring regarding praise and worship, I realize how necessary it is to really understand the absolutes of this dynamic message.

As we understand the absolutes of praise, I am convinced we will enter into even greater dimensions of worship, which in turn will produce a conclusive enjoyment and maturity in our walk with Christ.

What is praise and what is worship?

TWO KINDS OF PRAISE

The principle definition of the word PRAISE in the Bible is the Hebrew word "halal," which means to be clear in sound, to shine, to make a show, to boast, to be clamorously foolish, to rave, to celebrate. *Praise is an expression of the soul.* That is, it directly involves our mind, our will and our emotions. The Psalmist David repeatedly stated that our soul is to bless the Lord (Psalm 103:1), boast in the Lord (Psalm 34:2) and praise the Lord (Psalm 146:1). This expression of the soul is to manifest itself in many ways, as is seen in the Word of God. These ways include:

> SINGING Psalm 47:6,7
> SHOUTING Psalm 47:1
> CLAPPING OF HANDS Psalm 47:1
> LIFTING OF HANDS Psalm 134:2
> DANCING Psalm 150:4
> BOWING Psalm 95:6
> MUSICALLY Psalm 150

There have been times when these expressions have come automatically, spontaneously. Even though we may not have understood why, there was no hesitation in our response. But then there were other times when praise was the last thing we wanted to do, so we didn't. Unfortunately, by acting, or rather reacting only according to our feelings, we rob ourselves of real fulfilment in another aspect of praise — the SACRIFICE. What is spontaneous and what is sacrificial praise?

SPONTANEOUS PRAISE

David exhorts us in Psalm 103 to praise the Lord because of what He has done. Just think! He:

1. Forgives *all* our iniquities (v. 3)
2. Heals *all* our diseases (v. 3)
3. Redeems our life from destruction (v. 4)
4. Crowns us with lovingkindness and tender mercies (v. 4)
5. Satisfies our mouth with good things (v. 5).

Don't forget His benefits!

As we realize what a mighty God He is and what He has

done for us, we are stirred emotionally. Our feelings are touched in a dynamic way and we spontaneously erupt with praise! *Spontaneous praise is therefore BIRTHED IN OUR EMOTIONS. We feel* like praising the Lord! The emotional response is overwhelming; it bursts out of us like gushing water. Spontaneous praise is enjoyable, emotional, brimming with enthusiasm. And rightly so! We should praise the Lord *for* all He has done.

But, as I have already mentioned, what about the *other* times?

SACRIFICIAL PRAISE

Hebrews 13:15 exhorts us to offer the "sacrifice" of praise to God continually. The word "sacrifice" means the action of slaughtering, killing, or slaying. In other words, we are required to kill those emotions, slaughter those feelings that are *opposed* to praising the Lord. Many times I don't *feel* like praising the Lord. It is during those times that I can fulfil my obedience to Scripture and exercise the "Sacrifice of Praise."

Sacrificial praise is not birthed in our emotions. Sacrificial praise is *BIRTHED IN OUR WILL!* The most repeated phrase in the Psalms is "I will." In fact this phrase is repeated over 200 times! The Key of David is not to praise the Lord just when we feel like it, but also includes entering into the realms of sacrifice — willingly slaying our feelings and praising the Lord. *I WILL* praise the Lord. Even when I don't *feel* like it, *I WILL.* Even when circumstances don't stir me to, *I WILL.*

This aspect of praise is so important and so powerful that it enables us to enter a greater dimension of praise than even Lucifer, the anointed cherub, the chief musician of the heavens, could, in the beginning. Ezekiel 28:12-19 and Isaiah 14:12-14 tell us that Lucifer (whose name in Hebrew — "heylel" — is a derivative of the word praise), was *created* perfection. But iniquity was found in him; he failed to perfect himself *willfully.* He said, *"I will* exalt myself, *I will* ascend..." He acted on his emotions of pride — how he felt — and refused to enter into the aspect of sacrificial praise. The result was destruction and downfall. But thank God, today there are people who are beginning to understand and enter into sacrificial praise, people who are saying *"I WILL"* praise the Lord and are maturing in the realms of *willful* perfection.

The results of both spontaneous and sacrificial praise are awesome! God *responds* to praise! Psalms 22:3 tells us that He *inhabits*, He *dwells* in the praises of His people. And as a result of God's response, something supernatural takes place. We transcend from the dimension of praise into the dimension of worship.

THE DIMENSION OF WORSHIP

Whereas PRAISE is an expression of the SOUL, *WORSHIP is an EXPRESSION OF THE SPIRIT.* The word "worship" in the Hebrew is "shachah," which means to depress, prostrate, bow (self) down, crouch, fall down (flat), humbly beseech, do obeisance, do reverence, make to stoop. In the Greek the word is "proskuneo," which means to kiss, to fawn or crouch to, to revere, to adore. By this we can see that in worship there is a Divine, intimate communion, a closeness of relationship that occurs between God and man, the Creator and the created. Worship cannot be of the body because God is not a body. Worship cannot be of the soul, because God is not a mind, a will, an emotion. Worship is an *expression of the spirit,* because *"God is a Spirit: and they that worship him MUST worship him in spirit and in truth"* (John 4:24).

As we spontaneously and sacrificially praise the Lord we are lifted into the realm of the spirit, where a pure, holy, love relationship is developed with God. God *communes* with us and we commune with God. At that moment of transcension, you realize that you are on holy ground. Time is of no importance. Nothing else matters but your communion with God.

139

You are intensely aware of the fact that you are communing with God in spirit.

As you worship the Lord, He reveals Himself to you in a precious, loving way. As the definition, "to kiss" suggests, there results an intimate spiritual union with the Spirit of God. There is a strengthening, a refreshing that occurs in your spirit. You know you have met with God and God has met with you! Nothing can be compared to that type of communion, which is a result of your spontaneous and sacrificial praise.

I look back and count my blessings of growing up in this atmosphere of praise and worship. I give sincere thanks to Pastor Layzell, to my father and to all those who lifted my hands for me.

But even greater than the joy I feel in my own personal experience, is the joy I feel in seeing the awakening of this message around the world. Today, we are seeing a fulfilment of John 4:23:

"But the hour cometh and NOW IS, when the true worshippers shall worship the Father in spirit and in truth: for the Father SEEKETH such to worship him."

FOLLOW
THE LEADER
by Clement J. Ferris

Have you ever noticed how easily a group of enthusiastic youngsters respond to such childhood games as "Simon Says" or "Mother-May-I"? An equally popular pastime for playground pals would be the old time favorite "Follow the Leader." Now the key to any successful game of follow the leader is usually a direct result of the enthusiasm and creativity of the leader himself. Certainly you can recall those particular moments when your favorite leader had your undivided attention and anticipation while you had full confidence that he knew exactly where he was going. Does this sound like a Sunday morning service at your local church?

WHAT ARE THE RULES
The success and ultimate enjoyment of any group activity (like a game) depends on a clear set of guidelines or rules. The absence of such would result in chaos and confusion, not to

141

mention a lack of participation. Perhaps you have even experienced those who change the rules as the game goes along. Of course, you realize by now, that this has nothing to do with that unique portion of our church services many refer to as "praise and worship" — or does it?

Let's bring these situations into focus with a short scenario. Don Denomination has finally mustered up enough holy boldness to attend the church service of his persistent charismatic co-worker. Typically, he resigns himself to go to the evening service to escape the peer pressure of a morning worship service. Yes, Mr. Denomination is about to mount "a horse of a different color" that will take him down a pentecostal pathway never journeyed before! Don's first dilemma occurs when he notices there are no hymns posted in triplicity on either wall of the sanctuary. That's right, Don. Different church, different rules. Too embarrassed to inquire, he breaks into a cold sweat when he further discovers there aren't even any hymnals. As he scans his surroundings, the presence of electronic instruments and trap drums adds further trauma.

But wait! What's that bright light that just flashed in the corner? Why it's a projector screen with words in poetic form, accompanied by a burst of music and, finally, the appearance of an "announcer" to hopefully tell Don how to participate in this unorthodox worship experience. For the first time in his entire church life, Don Denomination must undergo congregational singing, stripped of his familiar surroundings and accompaniments, with all attention and trust in a stranger with a microphone who acts like the whole procedure is quite normal!

Many of us were perhaps relatives in the Denomination family who ventured into these unconventional worship experiences. Through much observation and teaching, coupled with trial and error, we have developed the ability to follow the leader and begun to deepen our perception of God's presence in worship.

"FOLLOW ME"

One of the most powerful commands Jesus spoke in the New Testament was simply, "Follow me." Thus, a true follower of Jesus is, by definition, "one going in the same way" from the Greek word "akolouthos." Acknowledging the scriptural principle of following, we can see the tremendous potential in worship when God's people all begin to "go in the same way." Paramount to participating in congregational worship is a submissive attitude in the worshipper's heart to follow the appointed worship leader for that particular worship service.

God's response to an obedient heart is promised in John 14:21, *"He that hath my commandments and keepeth them, he it is that loveth me: and he that loveth me shall be loved of my Father and I will love him and will MANIFEST myself to him."* As a worshipper ascends spiritually in his love and adoration for God, there will come a point where God's presence will manifest and begin to meet his needs on the spot (healing, deliverance, refreshing, etc.).

In Revelation chapter 14, we attain insight into the heavenly chorus depicted as the *"voice of many waters, a great thunder and harpers harping with their harps"* (vs. 2). They are described as singing a new song before the throne (v. 3); but the overall identify of such heavenly harmony is characterized for us in verse four. *"These are they which follow the Lamb withersoever he goeth."* One might say, "I would most gladly and easily follow Jesus into worship, but sometimes it seems like the worship leader begins doing his own thing and it just hinders my 'personal' flow of worship." If such "interference" is a problem that you or others might experience, then I would recommend a few areas of self-examination. First, check your level of heart submission to the appointed leadership for worship. (Do you ever pray for the worship team before a service, or are you just concerned that you will receive a spiritual blessing?) Secondly, realize that a true follower of Jesus expresses his obedience to Christ's universal church within the framework of a local church. Without covering the whole area of submission to church authority, I simply conclude that a believer's attitude toward God-appointed worship leaders will directly affect the levels of worship and blessing available in the corporate setting. Keep in mind that there are no perfect churches — only perfecting churches! The church is painfully learning the consequences of following a man or a ministry. God's desire for pure worship lies in a balance between a heart that yearns to follow after Him and a will that cooperatively submits to local church leadership.

MONKEY SEE MONKEY DO

Another precious quality that children often exhibit is the innate ability to imitate certain personalities and actions that impress or somehow stimulate their little minds. One of the Greek words for "follow" is "mimeomai," which is where we get the word "mimic." Simply put, we are exhorted to imitate God and His appointed leaders. Ephesians 5:1 says, *"Be ye therefore followers (imitators) of God."* We also have the apostle Paul admonishing us in I Corinthians 11:1, *"Be ye followers (imitators) of me, even as I also am of Christ."* If we apply these scriptures to our times of worship under anointed leadership, we can begin to enter God's presence by trusting the gift of God in the appointed leader for that service and just imitating his actions and directives. Sometimes it is much easier for us to follow (imitate) a worship leader or worship team when they all begin to lift their hands before the people or enthusiastically enter into a time of celebration and dancing.

Now there is only one method of imitation that is tried and proven to meet the expectations of Davidic worship. We must imitate in FAITH! The Beck translation of Hebrews 13:7 says it this way: *"Remember your leaders who told you God's Word.*

Consider how their lives ended and IMITATE THEIR FAITH."
It is a clear Biblical principle to imitate our leaders and, rest
assured, the worship leader himself is blazing a trail to the
throne with all the faith he can invoke! We need to press into
the direction of worship with the same fervent faith, making
spiritual ascent and gaining victory over the flesh.

A good example of one who refused to exercise faith to
imitate Davidic worship was none other than King David's
wife, Michal. *"And it came to pass, as the ark of the covenant of
the Lord came to the city of David, that Michal, the daughter of
Saul looking out at a window saw King David dancing and
playing: and she despised him in her heart"* (I Chronicles 15:29).
What is so clearly illustrated here in I Chronicles is a very real
conflict between the flesh and the spirit of many sincere worshippers today. Throughout the scriptures, David represents
the man of the spirit, while Saul portrays the man after the
flesh. Here we have King David rejoicing and dancing before
the Lord with abandon. This is the picture of God's true worshipper, releasing genuine praise from his spirit. At the same
time, we see Michal, the daughter of Saul (the flesh), looking
at this display of absolute faith toward God, yet refusing to
imitate God's chosen leader (even her own husband). Friends,
sometimes the worship leader will exhort you in the dance
before God and your flesh will despise the very thought of
dancing! Notice carefully the fate of Michal.

With this same account recorded in the sixth chapter of II
Samuel, God gives us something to consider in verse 23 as we
examine Michal's response to Davidic worship: *"Therefore
Michal the daughter of Saul had no child unto the day of her
death."* Because of her refusal to follow Israel's worship leader
and step out in faith, God caused her life to be barren — a
disgrace for any woman in those days, especially a queen.
Today, many believers are suffering from spiritual barrenness,
yet refuse to follow the leading of God's spirit in times of

corporate worship. God wants you fruitful! Dare to step out in faith and worship as David did!

WHERE ARE WE GOING?

For many Christians, the "trying of our faith" that James mentions in chapter one of his epistle can sometimes include a grueling contest of Sunday-morning Olympics, better known as "getting ready for church." We all know how the enemy tries to put us through the "agony of defeat" before we even set foot out the door! With steadfast perseverance and overcoming faith, we finally proceed down the road declaring, "Praise God! We're going to church."

Unfortunately, this proclamation is a self-contained goal for many in the church community today. Is it enough to say that we just "went to church" on Sunday? Is a padded pew or an altar rail our only intrinsic value? Are we merely people of destination without expectation?

Looking to the sixth chapter of Isaiah for reference, I believe a major focal point for today's worshipper rests in the ability to embrace an image of God birthed in revelatory worship. God's worship leader today must be one who attentively waits on the quickening of the Holy Spirit to launch God's people into a realm of prophetic revelation through high worship. The congregational worshipper must follow faithfully, anticipating a manifestation of God's presence in his midst. It is there, in habitation with the Father, that the images of our spiritual vision are brought into divine focus. This is what the prophet Isaiah experienced in worship as God totally transformed his vision, bringing conviction and repentance to release Isaiah into further prophetic ministry. Ultimately, where we are going for God is determined by our vision. True worship will focus your vision.

WHAT DO YOU SEE?

"In the year that king Uzziah died I saw also the Lord sitting

upon a throne, high and lifted up and his train filled the temple" (Isaiah 6:1). Under Uzziah, Judah experienced prosperity second only to Solomon. As young Isaiah witnessed this rapid development under Uzziah, his vision became distorted as the image of the natural kingdom he dwelled in took preeminence. In fact, it is recorded in II Chronicles 26:22 that Isaiah, perhaps so impressed with the potentate, wrote all the acts of Uzziah, "first and last."

As we examine the Isaiah worship phenomenon, phase one incorporates the death of the earthly image before the birthing of the heavenly. To adequately follow Christ into the depths of God's presence, any earthly (false) image of your worship must die! Throughout scripture, God deals in images and likeness. In order for the true image to replace the false, the false one has to be removed. For Isaiah, it was Uzziah. When our earthly images and idols die, God will come in and refocus our heavenly vision as we are led into His presence through worship.

Phase two depicts the reconstruction of Isaiah's vision as God reveals himself sitting on a throne (the true king), high and lifted up (in our worship). As Isaiah sets his focus on God, he receives a visual experience of God's glory, ushered in by the presence of the seraphims. In a tremendously powerful exchange of worship between the seraphs, there is a release of God's glory. *"In a great antiphonal chorus they sang, 'Holy, holy, holy is the Lord of Hosts; the whole earth is filled with His glory.' Such singing it was! It shook the Temple to its foundations and suddenly the entire sanctuary was filled with smoke."* (Isaiah 6:3,4 TLB) In what seems a paradox, the glory cloud brings a divine focus to the objectives and destinies of God. This manifestive sensation elicits a recognition and acknowledgment of Isaiah's inadequate representation of the image and likeness of God.

Worship leaders and followers alike — take heart to Isaiah's lamentation in verse five of chapter six: *"Then said I, Woe is me! for I am undone..."* What Isaiah had been projecting was less than the image of God's perfection ("... Holy, holy, holy ...") and his level of focus measured sensually low. May our cries of worship and exaltation of His glory bring an Isaiah response in our hearts to set the stage for a release of God's transforming power!

A worship leader in God's house has the responsibility to be an image bearer before God's people. The declaration of God's holiness and glory by the seraphim brought brokenness and an opening up of Isaiah's spirit before the throne. Please! We must understand that we are not competing with the world for a football stadium response. God wants the acknowledgment of our sins to the spirit of judgment and burning as found in Isaiah 4:4,5.

Notice the sequence following Isaiah's response. Isaiah SAW the Lord (v. 1,5). He admitted where he was, had his vision corrected, then HEARD the voice of God (v. 8). As with Isaiah, God often speaks to us in questions to help us identify where we really are, so that we can receive the grace to bring us where we need to be. Are you hearing God's voice as you worship Him? Many can hear God's voice, but they don't understand what He is saying. Babies hear the voice of their mother, but don't necessarily understand the words she is speaking. It is time for the body of Christ to "grow up" into mature, consecrated Isaiah worshippers. In verse nine, the Lord identifies Israel's hindrances in their worship: hearing, but not understanding; seeing, but not perceiving. Could these same hindrances be plaguing the church today?

What then is our objective in worship? What is the exchange taking place between heaven and earth when we come into His presence? May we have leaders who seek to bear God's image before the people and may we all follow the paths of praise set before us with submissive hearts and a spirit of unity.

When we begin to align ourselves to the heavenly image, as Isaiah of old, we will receive the same revelations as the mighty prophet and begin to fulfill God's prophetic purposes for our lives. Yes, follow the leader and become Isaiah worshippers that *"see with their eyes and hear with their ears and understand with their hearts"* (Isaiah 6:10).

WANTED:
CHRIST-LIKE MUSICIANS
by J. Mark Witt

S everal years a good friend of mine, who is a very talented musician, got married. A few months later I asked his wife a question that many newlyweds are asked: "How's married life treating you?" The answer she gave me took me quite by surprise and gave me much food for thought — "If I had it to do all over again, I would never marry a musician!"

Let's face it: That's a shame! However, in a good many cases musicians are just like that. They can be very hard "pills" to swallow.

There comes a time when, as musicians, we need to face a few issues. Why is it that musicians are so well known for their antics? Why is it that musicians are so hard to get along with? And why is it that we get branded as the "rabblerousers"?

Sometime back I was asked to speak to a group of musicians in Monterrey, Mexico. One of the topics I was asked to deal with was "The Life of the Musician." As I was thinking along that line, I wrote out a list of nine positives and nine negatives in the lives of most musicians. Please understand that I am generalizing here, but accept the challenge nonetheless.

POSITIVES

+ Sensitive/tender
+ Zealous
+ Hungry to learn
+ Not satisfied with the "status quo"
+ Expressive
+ Persistent (not quitters)
+ Good leaders
+ Positive thinkers ("dreamers"/visionaries)
+ Perfectionists

NEGATIVES

- Temperamental
- Self-centred (egotists)
- Self-assured (this could be positive if used correctly)
- Impatient
- Perfectionists (to the extreme of being fastidious)
- Unteachable (want to learn it all on their own)
- Jealous
- Moody/volatile
- Unstable/indecisive

I'm sure there are more we could add on both sides, but this is just a brief look at some of the major attitudes we deal with.

Too many people allow us to "get by" with our bad attitudes because of the way we play or sing. They say, "Oh, how can such singing/playing not be anointed!?" And we are just as carnal when we allow our talents to be used as a cover-up for our bad attitudes.

It is unfortunate that on many occasions a musician is received just because his talent is well-developed and impressive, even though as far as Christian character is concerned there is little or no development. I am not a believer in that mentality. If a musician can't live up to the basic standards laid down in the Word of God, he shouldn't be ministering in the house of the Lord as a Levite!

In Amos 6:1,3-6 we see a picture of some musicians who are obviously taking advantage of a certain group of people — the "young of the flock": *"Woe to them...that lie upon beds of ivory and stretch themselves upon their couches and eat the lambs of the flock and the calves out of the midst of the stall; that chant to the sound of the viol and invent to themselves instruments of musick..."* Here is a prime example of musicians using their God-given gifts in negative ways.

You see, we are all leaders to somebody, though many of us would rather not have that responsibility. Somebody out there is really listening to us and hanging on every word we say or sing. That is one good reason why our life has to meet up to God's standards. Too often we excuse ourselves with one of the typical pat answers: "Well, that's the way I've always been," or that all-time favourite, "You've got to accept me for what I am, brother." Sorry! The Word of God says that if anyone is in Christ, that person leaves all those "old" things behind (works of the flesh, Galatians 5:19-21) and from there on, everything is to become "new" (fruits of the Spirit, Galatians 5:22-23). The fruits of the Spirit can be expected to develop in our lives.

I believe that the spirit of the musician is expressed in his music. So if the spirit is carnal, the music — the "fruit" — will be likewise. Christ did say that we would be recognized by our fruit. Therefore, it is important that the fruit of our gift be in line with the fruit of the Spirit, so that those who listen will be edified.

For us Levites, on whose shoulders rests the responsibility

of carrying the ark of God's presence, it is time to face up to these issues. We must deal with these areas in our lives in order to increase our effectiveness in carrying God's presence to the people. It is time to start turning the tables, to make ourselves more of a blessing to the people around us. I have been told that people can't even stand to be around certain Christian musicians! This has to change! It's up to you and me.

What are you going to do when situations bring out those bad attitudes in your life? Are you just going to "let it ride," or will you accept the challenge and let yourself be changed by the Holy Spirit? We need to separate ourselves from what is considered to be normal in musicians and turn those negatives into positives. Notice on the preceding list that almost all the negatives can be linked to a corresponding positive. So allow God to speak to you and let's give people a reason to start liking the person we have become, not just the talent we have.

The Church of the Firstborn and The Birthright — by Kevin J. Conner (Victoria, Australia). This is an outstanding presentation of the "first-born" theme which runs from Genesis to Revelation. Kevin Conner, a widely recognized, anointed Bible teacher, examines the implications of questions such as: "Is the Church of the Firstborn (Hebrews 12:23) any church, or is it some distinctive church? What is the birthright of the Christian and can he sell it as the Hebrew believers were tempted to do?"

The Christian School Booklet — co-authored by Dr. Chris Gerrard (Saskatoon, Sask., Canada) and Pastor Dave Wells (Regina, SK, Canada). The disturbing and devastating effects of an educational system which shuts out Christ are apparent from every perspective in our day. Humanism has made damaging inroads, particularly in the field of education. This booklet points out the negative influence of humanism and powerfully presents the need for schools that are Biblically based.

The Prophecy/Presbytery Book — co-authored by Dr. David K. Blomgren (Tampa, Florida, U.S.A.) and Rev. Daniel Straza (Regina, Sask., Canada). In this booklet, Dr. Blomgren examines such areas as "What is Prophecy?" and "Judging the Prophetic Word," and looks at the differences between the "spirit" of prophecy, the "gift" of prophecy and the "office of a prophet." Rev. Straza sheds some light on the relatively unknown ministry of presbytery and its purpose in the local church. He also answers questions concerning "How to prepare for a Presbytery," and "How to respond to a word given in Presbytery." If you are interested in attending or having a presbytery meeting, or if you sense God is stirring you in the area of prophecy, then this booklet is for you!

For information and a complete list of publications produced
or distributed by our ministry, write:

Trumpet Publications
3920 S. Kings Avenue
Brandon, FL 33511
U.S.A.

You may photocopy form for re-use

ORDER FORM

For Phone Orders Call:
717-532-3040 or
FAX 717-532-9291

Return with your check or M.O. to Destiny Image, P.O. Box 351, Shippensburg, PA 17257

QTY.	DESCRIPTION	UNIT PRICE	TOT. PRICE

Ship. (quant.)	1-2	3-5	6-9	10-14	15-19	20-25
Ship. Cost	$1.75	$2.95	$4.95	$7.75	$9.95	$12.00

Name _____

Address _____

City/State/ZIP _____

Date _____ Phone# _____

SUBTOTAL _____

LESS DISCOUNT _____

SHIPPING _____

TOTAL DUE _____

Restoration
TODAY
Magazine

"Restoration Today Magazine" is an inspirational, Bible-teaching magazine published quarterly by Tampa Bay Christian Center and Trumpet Publications in Brandon, Florida, U.S.A. Reaching into more than eighty countries, the goal of this publication is to strengthen the body of Christ worldwide. Articles deal with subjects which are being emphasized by the Holy Spirit in the present move of God — unity, praise and worship, family life. The Tabernacle of David, supportive ministry, etc. These writings are submitted by proven ministries from North America and around the world.

If you desire to establish present truth in your own heart, in your local church and in the lives of those around you, "Restoration Today Magazine" can be a help to you.

Since this ministry operates on a donation basis, there is no set subscription rate. Please write:

"Restoration Today Magazine"
3920 S. Kings Avenue
Brandon, Florida 33511
U.S.A.